JOHN A. WILLIAMS is a s⸏⸏⸏⸏ study of John Williams, best ⸏ *Man Who Cried I Am, Sissie,* *God Didn't Save.* This book tra⸏ black writer's literary developm⸏ sophical concepts, provides valuable insight into his writings and presents a ⸏⸏⸏⸏ ⸏⸏

THIRD PRESS LIBRARY OF CRITICISM

General Editor: Joseph Okpaku

2
JOHN A. WILLIAMS:
THE EVOLUTION OF
A BLACK WRITER

The Third Press Library of Criticism

1. James Baldwin: A Critical Study—Stanley Macebuh
2. John A. Williams: The Evolution of a Black Writer—Earl Cash

FORTHCOMING
Critical studies on:

Wole Soyinka
Chinua Achebe
Ralph Ellison
Additional titles to be announced

JOHN A. WILLIAMS: THE EVOLUTION OF A BLACK WRITER

by Earl A. Cash

THE THIRD PRESS
Joseph Okpaku Publishing Company, Inc.
444 Central Park West, New York, N.Y. 10025

Library of Congress Catalog Card Number: LC73-92796
ISBN 0-89388-142-2

First printing

Designed by Bennie Arrington

To Eric B. Cash

ACKNOWLEDGMENTS

For the use of copyrighted material in this book grateful acknowledgment is made to the following:

Black World, for permission to include an interview with Williams from its June 1973 issue;

Cooper Square Publishers, for permission to quote from *Africa: Her History, Lands and People* copyright © 1963, by John A. Williams;

Coward-McCann & Geoghegan, Inc., for permission to quote from *The King God Didn't Save* copyright © 1970, by John A. Williams;

Doubleday & Co., Inc., for permission to include "We Regret to Inform You That" from *Flashbacks* copyright © 1972, and excerpts from *Captain Blackman* copyright © 1972, *The Most Native of Sons* copyright © 1970, by John A. Williams;

Little, Brown & Co., for permission to quote from *The Man Who Cried I Am* copyright © 1967, by John A. Williams;

The David McKay Co., for permission to quote critical remarks about *The Angry Ones;*

John A. Williams, for permission to quote from *The Angry Ones* copyright. © 1960, *Night Song* copyright © 1961, *Sissie* copyright © 1963, *This Is My Country Too* copyright © 1965, and *Sons of Darkness, Sons of Light* copyright © 1969.

THE AUTHOR WISHES TO THANK THE FOLLOWING:

The Ford Foundation, for a research fellowship;

The Graduate Student Allocations Committee at The University of New Mexico, for travel funds;

Syracuse University, for the use of the John A. Williams Collection at the George Arents Research Library;

Special thanks to John A. Williams for his untiring assistance, to R. Fleming, B. R. Hewins, L. Rhone, A. Gayle, C. A. Cash, J. A. Rahming, and M. G. Feliciano.

Contents

		Page
	Introduction	1
ONE:	The Man and His Nonfiction	11
TWO:	Tainted Chicken: *The Angry Ones*	33
THREE:	No Sambo Smiles: *Night Song*	47
FOUR:	Aunt Jemima is Dead: *Sissie*	73
FIVE:	A Black Act: *The Man Who Cried I Am*	97
SIX:	The Hymn of Return: *Sons of Darkness, Sons of Light*	109
SEVEN:	Uncle Sam's Gratitude: *Captain Blackman*	117
EIGHT:	Conclusion	125
NINE:	Appendix	131
	Selected Bibliography	163
	Index	165

Introduction

From the inception of the novel, a tension existed, as it did in other literary genres and art forms, between subjective and objective rendering of events. In response to the romantic and stream of consciousness fictions emerged the realistic and naturalistic. At the turn of the century, Hamlin Garland, Stephen Crane, Jack London, Frank Norris, Upton Sinclair and Theodore Dreiser—all in the name of objectivity—unsettled American fiction by portraying therein the squalid appetites of man, unleashed amidst a predatory environment that bartered humanity for survival. Implicitly, at least, these writings protested the apparent rambling impressionism of a Joyce, Proust, Virginia Woolf as well as the "moral" stories of a Hawthorne, Dostoevsky, or Samuel Clemens. When Blacks wrote, they fell instinctively into the naturalists' camp. Because of social circumstances they had little time for forms which glossed, shrouded, romanticized (though there would be black romantics) their concerns. Startlingly, their white counterparts did not rush to welcome them to the fold. In the nineteenth century, Whites reacted with amusement to a *Clotel,* with disregard to a *Blake,* and with malignant neglect to *Imperium in Imperio.* To such treatment would be added, in the present century, the charge of parochialism and acute subjectivism. As in social matters so it is in the literary: race became an inevitable determinant. What by a white writer was naturalism became by a Black self-serving, paranoid exaggerations.

It is important to understand the reason for this double standard toward black achievement. However, to understand is not to excuse. Success of the American Revolution paved the way for the realization of new hopes and dreams by early settlers. They had come to America to escape Old World tyranny. Once here and once independent, they had a second chance. America became in fact a new paradise, a heaven on earth. And to soothe those whose existence missed the blissful mark, the greatest con game of all times was invented—the American dream, a dictum of infinite possibilities. Under this umbrella nothing is unat-

1

tainable. Mix with such a dream a work ethic, a Puritan ethic, then the most bizarre potpourri materializes. Good forever will conquer evil, diligence and hard work will fashion the most inept into the stuff of presidents, and the meek shall inherit the earth. Whatever its inconsistencies, this credo demands and receives unshakable belief and is paid true homage.

But a price had to be paid for transgressing the First Commandment. Consequently, the inflexibility of Americans in accepting as gospel their man-made precepts led repeatedly to disasters. Perseverance with highest moral fortitude often did not bring success. Worse still, the achievement of success did not guarantee happiness, the ultimate end of the American dream. Rather, the American tragedy is that no matter how fatuous the national dream, no matter how many times it has proved to create more problems than it solves, the American clings all the harder to it. Some observers have termed this phenomenon the American innocence. Indeed, it may have been a type of naiveté (America was never innocent) on the part of those who earlier sailed to these shores from Europe, but once these groups who coveted religious freedom became intolerant of other sects, once they established an oligarchical government under the guise of democracy and theocracy, once they denied rights and freedom to all men, naiveté could no longer explain their behavior. For it was out-and-out conscious hypocrisy. Still, the conscience had to be assuaged, a rationale had to be found; thus surfaced a "justification" that has reverberated from the shores of the U.S. throughout the decades and centuries: Whatever wrongs done by and weaknesses of America (many would admit to neither), the country remained, nevertheless, the mightiest, morally and militarily, and there existed the greatest level of opportunity in the world. How many wars, murders, suicides, how much insanity, hatred, disillusionment—in short, what unimaginable numbers must endure physical or spiritual deaths in preserving a fabrication?

One lesson the American politician of any worth learns quickly is the penchant of the country for deception. No wonder an honest politician becomes a contradiction of terms, especially one who truly represents the people. Yet, deceiving others begins to be, in translation, self-deception; the first is immoral, the second pathetic. If, as Christ submitted, those who have not seen but still believed are blessed, surely

2

America is damned for shutting its eyes so it cannot see the truth about itself; surely by this very act America is its own slavemaster. Like a true tyrant it will permit no dissent, hastily buying off those who can be bought, murdering those who cannot. Its artists have long ago realized their limits. Products and victims of their society, they have shared in deflecting their audience from the false foundation on which the country rests. For pieces of silver writers have written tales about war and violence abroad as opposed to the horrors here, about technological worlds of the future instead of the present world of sterility, about twentieth century man glorified in his alienation rather than about his strangulation because of it.

When the black writer, a social outcast because of race—no insistence to the contrary will alter this fact—outlines in his tale the specifics of his deplorable condition, the poverty, sickness, discrimination, and sometime joys, white America, in refusing to confront the truth underlying the literature, in flaying the writing as subjective and paranoid, remains religious to its habit of self-imposed myopia. Just as white America has made historical buffoons out of Blacks, the white literary critics make fools out of black storytellers. Paul Laurence Dunbar used white characters in all but one of his many novels, Sutton Griggs took an accomodationist stance, James Weldon Johnson published his first novel anonymously, Charles Chesnutt abandoned writing for law, Jean Toomer wrote allegorically, Claude McKay celebrated the black low-life and received criticism from Blacks, Wallace Thurman wrote on intra-racial prejudice and received criticism from Blacks, Richard Wright expostulated against racial inequities and received criticism from Blacks. The point is that black writers either reacted to their white critics, or to a black audience which internalized the white posture or to the pressure of white controlled economics.

The same William Dean Howells who lavished praise on Crane's *Maggie: A Girl of the Streets* would decry as bitter Chesnutt's *The Marrow of Tradition*. The same Stanley Edgar Hyman who praised Richard Wright would complain that Ralph Ellison was not sufficiently like Wright. What other recourse did the black writer have save the announcing of a black aesthetic? Pity it should have taken him so long.

An urging of literary self-determination, the black aesthetic has been

3

applauded by some and denounced by others. Certainly it threatens the influence of white critics who for so long have seen to it that only one black writer be recognized at a time. For these same critics, Wright, Ellison and Baldwin comprise all the black novelists of this century; others receive no mention because of ignorance or because of an unwillingness to alter the one-black-writer-at-a-time syndrome. With curious desperation, the white critics are now playing catch-up. They see their powers waning and this they must avoid at any cost, even if it means having to study those heretofore non-existent novelists. They will not let blacks establish and monopolize a market for articles on black literature, even if it means studying this literature under black tutelage; hence the amazing, infectious rash of white theses and dissertations on black writers.

Already proponents of a black aesthetic have been charged with creating a literary isolationism. Black writers and critics must not be seduced by such a ploy; isolationistic or not, they must view white criticism with a scepticism warranted by history. The black novelist, for example, should write stories dealing with non-black problems without fearing the reproof of trespassing or being a traitor. Since the purpose of a black aesthetic is to afford freedoms and confidence to the artists, they should quickly slip the bonds of white critics who have directioned for too long the nature of their art. Nor should they relinquish one bondage for another; that is, they must beware relegating to black critics the previously held authority of white, because both have their treachery. Similarly, black critics should skirt the temptation, say, to denigrate a Frank Yerby for not being black enough and to deify a Robert Beck for glamorizing the world of pimps and prostitutes. The critical approach needs to be an inductive one, one in which the critics suspend preconceptions and biases, in order to be fair. Thus an onus falls on the black critic to excel where the white would not, to exhibit fair-mindedness where the other would be retarded by inbred racism.

To ask that the victims of dishonesty and mistreatment become models for fairness and moral integrity has to be ironic. Yet this is what it has come to, and Blacks may as well face a few facts; such as, they are black Americans, they share a belief in the American dream and have deeper roots in this country than they may care to admit. America

4

will never achieve the literary virtuosity of a Dostoevsky, Joyce, Mann or Kafka until its writers commit themselves to that reluctantly used word, truth. Because Whites have seldom risen to this challenge, it is incumbent upon black writers, whatever the irony, to do so. They must continue to depict with unflinching honesty the good, the bad, the canker of poverty, injustice, corruption, and the sustaining, vital hopes and dreams. If the great American novel has not already been written by a Black, it surely will be.

No writer, black or white, moves in a vacuum. Black writers have reflected the times with unparalleled openness and consistency. One can discern in the sixties the effects of black power (a social and political twin to the black aesthetic) on writers like William Melvin Kelley, John Oliver Killens, John A. Williams, and Ishmael Reed. What these novelists mirror is that Blacks are more American, ideally, than is America itself. Black people tend to place eternal store in the innate goodness of man, in the conviction that good ultimately demolishes evil. They are as much Utopia-seekers as anyone else; only they take their quest seriously. So the ambivalence which surrounds the black writers encircles Blacks on the whole. Both can see that America's flaw comes from not owning up to its weaknesses, from deluding itself that good triumphs. Yet, when Blacks search for a surrogate system, they propose one based even more heavily on the principles which have failed America. Black writers recognize the dual posture of black people: they have been kept out of the mainstream of American life long enough to see clearly its infested core; but they have been within the physical boundaries of this continent sufficiently long to believe that this system can work. Here is tragedy in its noblest form. And the nobility would be lost were Blacks to abandon hope, were they to cease trusting that as America goes so do Blacks; or likely, it is the other way around.

John A. Williams is one of numerous black authors whose books dotted the bookstore racks in the sixties and seventies. Having written fiction and nonfiction, he will survive as being foremost a novelist. He holds his own among the best American novelists of this century, but he has received scant recognition for varying reasons, many of which have been outlined here. What follows, therefore, should throw into perspective the iron backbone most black people must have. What

5

follows should elaborate why Williams is a writer to be reckoned with. Lastly, it should help stimulate an appreciation for the few writers who still try to convey the truth about America. While Williams is one such writer, the others are likely wallowing in obscurity because they, too, declined to barter their souls. This study should serve as a testimonial to those unknown persons of courage.

* * *

When Ace Publishing Company released a cheap paperback entitled *The Angry Ones* in 1960, it represented the anti-climax of years of writing, rewriting and frustrated hopes. Fortunately it represented also a turning point for a man who had just about decided that his calling lay outside the literary field. Encouraged, he immediately returned to work on a second novel and a nonfictional book about Africa. From then on John A. Williams would average a book a year.

John Alfred is the oldest of four children, two girls and two boys, by John Henry and Ola Williams. Mississippians and little over a generation removed from emancipation, the couple had settled north in Syracuse, New York, only to journey south once again in 1925 for the birth of John, who later would render this description of events:

> Jackson is my mother's birthplace, and was her home for a time. I was born there. My parents were married and made their home in Syracuse, where I was conceived (I refuse to give all my heritage to Mississippi), but they returned to Jackson for the birth of their first child, according to the custom of the time. Thus, in my family, a line of "free" Negroes on my father's side, and one of former "slave Negroes" on my mother's side were merged.[1]

Young John grew up in Syracuse, a booming industrial town that had managed to attract a large number of immigrants. He attended Washington Irving Elementary, Madison Junior High, and Central High School. As with many youngsters, adolescence for him had its joys and its burdens, and in retrospect they all jell to form a halo over the past that sanctifies equally the harsh and easy times. With nostalgia, Williams would recall:

6

I was raised in the 15th Ward and spent most of my life there
. . No where [sic] in Syracuse is change more obvious, for the
Ward has all but vanished . . . Yellow bulldozers groaned back
and forth over the scarred land making sure that every vestige of
the unhappy Negro who last inhabited the Ward is crushed out of
sight, out of memory.
But the Ward was not always black and it was not always unhappy.
Many kinds of people lived there, Negroes, Jews, Italians, Irish,
Poles, Indians and "native Americans." The people shared conversation and other small joys. The religious holidays of all were greatly
respected. If your parents were at work or shopping someone on
the block had his or her eye on you. In the Ward survival of the
other fellow and his children meant survival for you. For me, the
Ward was home and the rest of Syracuse radiated outward from
it. It was a city within a city and at dusk the year around, you
could see men of all sizes, shapes and colors returning to it from
their jobs, such as they were.[2]

World War II interrupted his high school education, for in 1943 he
joined the Navy where his duties included regimental bugler and pharma-
cist's mate. Disillusioned by racism in the service, he returned to Syracuse to get married in 1946 after honorable naval discharge. That same
year, he completed high school and enrolled at Syracuse University
The births of two sons, the receipt of a Bachelor's degree in Journalism
and English would highlight the next five years. Williams reconstructs
the following details of the fifties:

I graduated in June, 1950, and started graduate school (also at Syracuse
University, in English) right away. I came out of graduate school
January '51 and went to work in a foundry where I had worked
primarily before. Then I hurt my back (that same incident causes
me to use a brace every now and then); I couldn't do the job I
had been working on. I left there and became a clerk at Loblaw's
Supermarket on Adams Street. At this time they must have had
the most intellectual group of clerks in the city. They were trying
to do something, I suppose, democratic. But all of the black people
there had at least a Bachelor's degree and some had Master's. The

manager of the store tried to elicit from everyone a promise that they would spend the rest of their lives at Loblaw's. Of course, we all said yes.

In the meantime I put in an application for work as a caseworker at the Onondaga County Welfare Department. I think that came through in the Spring of '52; in any case, when I left Loblaw's I went to work for the County. I was a caseworker and had a mixed caseload: public assistance, ADC, old age and aid to the disabled—those four categories. Then I moved to the children's division, Children's Protective Service it was called. It was kind of a plush job. There was some question as to whether they wanted me there; there was some fear that I'd be raping mothers and stuff like that. Nobody ever bothered to worry about the mothers I had dealt with on a public role in the ADC category, mostly because, I guess, they were poorer than the people involved in the Children's Protective Service; they turned out in many cases to be just as poor but most of them [in ADC] were Blacks. Some of those cases were pretty grim.

Things had fallen finally apart with Carolyn [his wife] and I, and I left Syracuse the summer of '54 for California. I spent a year [in Los Angeles] looking for work. Then I got involved with a black outfit that was mainly a bunch of real estate hustlers and I still have the first penny to get from those people. Then some other hustlers wanted to start an employment agency. I wound up at Golden State Mutual, a life insurance company, and the pay was—well, it was terrible. Instead of paying you, all the officials of the company came around in the morning and shook your hand and called you mister. You had a meal ticket so you could get three lunches at cost during the week; the other days you were just pretty much on your ass. Finally I left there. I think they thought I had some skills because when I told them I was leaving to go back East, my boss called me in and asked why. I said I wanted to be close to my kids, which was true. But there was no point to discussing salary with those people because it was a very nepotistic outfit, controlled by three or four families. There just was no place in there for any outsider to really advance; particularly, I think, if you had talent,

8

they tended to be a little scared. So I came back East and started working in New York.[3]

Williams had begun in California and completed in 1956 in New York City what would become his first published novel. Between then and early 1960, he would sometimes find himself jobless and penniless. He produced and edited a public relations newsletter named *Negro Market Newsletter;* he worked in a publishing house and persisted in his writing and in his efforts to find a publisher.

Of the fourteen books by Williams, six are fiction, six nonfiction and two anthologies. A limited report on the nonfiction appears here first because it supplies a necessary background of information plus a valuable insight into the concerns of the author—concerns which repeatedly emerge in his fiction but are more outrightly elaborated in his nonfiction. For certain, an introduction to the nonfiction, despite the chronological jumps, supplies an ample prelude to Williams' fiction—the thrust of this study.

References

1. John A. Williams, *This Is My Country Too* (New York: Signet, 1966), pp. 70-71.
2. _____, "Syracuse: A City in Transition," an unpublished article in the John A. Williams Collection in the George Arents Research Library for Special Collections at Syracuse University.
3. From an interview with John A. Williams on September 28, 1973.

One

The Man and His Nonfiction

By 1963, John A. Williams had published two novels and expected the appearance of a third within a few months. Early in that year Cooper Square released *Africa: Her History, Lands and People*.[1] One reviewer labored to convey an idea of its content:

John A. Williams has just published the first paperback, illustrated history of Africa . . . has recreated the dramatic course of African history from the "first man" to the current strive [sic] for national independence . . . In the enlarged Fact finder [sic] each country is listed with its size, leaders, capital, products, resources, animal and plant life.[2]

Indeed, paraphrasing Williams' *Africa* presents a task because it is so deceptively simple yet saturated with vital information. For example, Africa signifies to many the primitive and untamed, and the author notes that *Zinjanthropus Boisei,* the earliest man, had been found there. However, during the sixteenth century the same wild country had universities, medical and law schools, with the greatest centers of learning at that time at Timbuktu.

Africa, therefore, lays out plainly a brief history of the continent, focusing on not-so-well-circulated facts. It outlines how Christopher Columbus can be held accountable for introducing slavery to Haiti, how Scottish explorer and missionary David Livingstone "unwittingly did more than anyone else to bring on the rush by European powers to grab colonies for themselves in Africa" (35), how slave rebellions occurred as early as 1522, refuting the myth of black docility. In short, the book demonstrates an interest in revealing historical truths which white historians had a vested interest in omitting. Significantly, Williams' study occurs before it became fashionable to see numerous texts on black history. In the last part of the sixties and in the seventies, Otto Lindenmeyer's *Black History: Lost, Stolen, or Strayed,* Tuesday Magazine's *Black Heroes in World History* and Benjamin Quarles' *The Negro in the Making of America* represent few of an almost overnight surge of titles reflecting on Blacks in history.

Knowing one's past is most essential if one is to be able to confront adequately one's present, Williams believes. And in *Africa: Her History, Lands and People,* a text designed to appeal to young readers, he exhibits his dedication to history. While each succeeding book will make some comment on the importance of discovering the truth of the past, none manifests so totally this importance as the author's first nonfictional effort on Africa.

*   *   *

Using a pseudonym, Williams co-authored *The Protectors*[3] in 1964, a book similar in tone to the popular television series "The FBI." Williams explains:

> The Protectors was published in April, 1964. I used a pseudomyn [sic]—J for John; Dennis for my youngest son; Gregory for my oldest son. I did not feel that I should use my name on this because it is not a novel and because I've never approved of all the methods used by the Narcotics Bureau. The methods I disliked you won't find here except between the lines where I managed to put them. However, and frankly, I had no quarrel with the money it paid; sad, but true.[4]

The text's full title is *"The Protectors: Our Battle Against the Crime Gangs* by Harry J. Anslinger, former U.S. Commissioner of Narcotics, with J. Dennis Gregory."* Accordingly, the stories in the book celebrate the narcotics agents as they crack case after case. Today, a similar work, no doubt, would be quickly dismissed as superficial. However, Anslinger took serious pride in his undercover agents, obsessed with getting the pusher, convinced that their being on the side of the law explained whatever methods or techniques they used, whatever hostile or inhumane treatment they inflicted. Although some sections, like the chapter which recounts the demise of black entertainers Billie Holiday and Charlie Parker, engage the reader, they do not allay the curiosity of the reader over how Williams happened to be associated with such a book and how much of it he did actually write. To the latter query, Williams responds that he wrote the entire book from material supplied by Anslinger:

> The cases are real cases, I just changed the names, but the material came from the files that Anslinger gave me. I had asked him to make sure that he gave me files on where the black agent and Jewish agent had been active. He said okay, and that's why we have those particular things in there.
>
> Also, I think I liked the guy, although I know he's got a terrible name. I slipped through some things there that he must have known about but never said anything about. For instance, there is quite a long section on the presence of narcotics clinics in the thirties in New York—the idea of establishing clinics is a position that the Feds have opposed for quite a while but had been very quiet about the fact that they had them at one time. Then there are two doctors who had the same name; one doctor was operating in the thirties another in the fifties; they're father and son and their views are totally different. But I'm sure Anslinger knew what I was doing and just chose to say nothing about it.
>
> Most of that stuff is pretty innocuous, if not funny, considering some of those shootouts they had in the Southwest chasing opium dealers, with everybody armed with forty-fives, shooting all over hell and not hitting a goddamn thing—that's pretty funny stuff.[5]

As to how Williams got involved with what might be considered such an off-beat project, two facts provide some insight. First, the pay for the writing attracted a man who though beginning to gain recognition as a writer received slight financial profit. A few years later he would write a novel with the same motive. So, when two black writers in one of his novels talk of producing "potboilers" in order to eat, their conversations take on extra weight because they suggest the author's own hard times. Second, the chance to review actual federal cases intrigued Williams. An opportunity to glimpse otherwise secret operations of the Narcotics Bureau was a rare one that had to be seized. The overall significance of his experience with *The Protectors* might be that it provided details for a narcotics chase in his most popular novel as well as information for articles on Holiday and Parker. Williams' claim that he used a pseudonym because the book was not a novel hardly convinces. He must have known that his association with Anslinger would make him vulnerable on a couple of fronts, and it must have occurred to him that he might have let himself in for surveillance of some kind or for being investigated to be cleared for the project. Williams stoutly affirms:

I had nothing to hide. One rumor coming out of the Prix de Rome thing [a writing award for which the author had been selected but subsequently was mysteriously rejected] was that I was mixed up in narcotics. If there had been any question about my having been involved with narcotics Anslinger would not have worked with me. I assume it's a matter of procedure that a man of that position checks out anybody he's going to work with. Now as for any additional surveillance for political matters, I don't know, but I'm sure that as far as any activities in narcotics usage or traffic, he must have had me checked out and found me to be absolutely clean.[6]

But even in 1964, a Black linked with the former U.S. Commissioner of Narcotics risked being seen by other Blacks as a turncoat and a threat. This may have been the underlying thought behind Williams using a pseudonym for his first and only time.

* * *

I have traveled in many parts of the world. In America I live in New York, or dip into Chicago or San Francisco. But New York is no more America than Paris is France or London is England. Thus I discovered that I did not know my own country.

So begins *Travels with Charley* by John Steinbeck. Subtitled "In Search of America,'' the book includes the impressions a seasoned writer like Steinbeck accrued during his drive through thirty-four states in 1961. Despite lapses, *Travels* obviously impressed enough people sufficiently to win the 1962 Nobel Prize for literature. The following year, *Holiday* magazine, hoping to capitalize on the success of Steinbeck's effort, commissioned John A. Williams to take a similar cross-country trip. His was to be a black version of *Travels*. Supplied with a new car and credit cards, Williams, in September 1963, was on his way. The results, serialized in *Holiday,* made up his third nonfictional book, somewhat defiantly titled *This Is My Country Too* (1965).[7]

In a style not unlike Steinbeck, Williams recorded conversations and experiences as he journeyed throughout the country. Also like Steinbeck, the trip became both a physical and spiritual one. At the end of it all, he left the United States for several months' travel in the Middle East and Africa, carrying with him a darker opinion of America. Yet, he had concluded his book with a note of hope even amidst a general despondency:

> I am committed to the search for its [America's] true meaning; I hope what I have found is not it. I am forced to hope for it and I have no choice but to meet the challenge of it. (158)

Recounting parts of the travel might explain the grim mood of the author at its conclusion.

He observes in Vermont a sluggish civil rights movement, in Kentucky beautiful landscapes which contrast with the ugliness of racial injustice. A visit with a talented friend in Nashville brings this revelation:

> No matter how much individual Negroes may achieve, it counts for nothing in the white community. (45)

At black colleges, he perceives the students' eager search for status through clothes, cars and friends. In his novels, Williams would protest repeatedly the traditional forms of security and status. *This Is My Country Too* registers forceful opposition to a mindless quest for what society dictates as desirable.

In North Dakota, a lieutenant greets him at an airbase with, "We don't have any racial problems here." Problems abound: black airmen receive the poorest housing; they get served at only a handful of restaurants in town; they get the stiffest sentences for the smallest infractions; they get no respect from white crewmen; their dating white women often results in physical attack by the white servicemen. Frustration and desperation pervade the base. Helpless, Williams calls *Jet* magazine and asks that they send a reporter to cover the conditions. Confronted by racism at the airbase the writer remembers his own troubles in the Navy:

First there was the segregated naval base at Great Lakes, Camp Robert Smalls, then the segregated units . . . My biggest battles, however, were not against the Japanese, but against the United States Navy and many of my white comrades. I had more fire then. I raised some little hell. I spent three hitches in the brig, one of them a Marine brig. I was usually charged with breaking some Navy regulation, but I was fighting for my rights as a sailor, black or not. I saw white Marines and black sailors line up for a race riot on Guam. A Chamorro girl told me that she had been warned to stay away from black men because they had tails. My parents wrote asking what was being cut out of my letters. I had endless conferences with the censors and refused to stop writing home and saying that the Navy was rotten. I have a pitted face from the dry shaves I got in the Marine brig. (13-14)

But all was not negative. Some people and some places brought encouragement. The author notes that in the South, human interaction did occur between the races.

Whites and blacks weren't continually at each others' throats; ....There was not the cleared space, the No Man's Land, the demilitarized zone. No, lives dovetailed. (79)

The truths which Williams discovered on his travel vary only in specifics and degree from those Steinbeck found. Whereas one moved in a white world, the other moved in a black. Still both apprehended a moral crisis, particularly when it came to civil rights. Both lay claim to America as being their country, whatever its faults. Steinbeck's claim, at any rate, was no mere wishful thinking.

Critical reception was predictable. Some critics reviewed *This Is My Country Too,* but its reception nowhere equaled *Travels with Charley.* Somehow a black man touring the country and taking its pulse interested few people. *Holiday* got its serialization; Williams reached a wider audience than he did with his earlier nonfictional works, yet no hurrahs and bravos were forthcoming. When *Reader's Digest* in 1973 asked Williams to take another tour and he refused, maintaining he had neither time nor the energy, he must have asked himself what's the use—outside of his own personal gain.

Some discoveries the author makes may seem dated and well-known. Remembering the tremendous change in race awareness since 1963 and '64 should explain this impression. Williams was realizing then what many other Blacks at that time began to realize and what is now accepted as fact:

a great majority of white people have no intention of sharing with black people what we have called the American dream—unless they are forced to. (157)

Parts of the book may also draw a charge of being erratic as paragraphs switch from serious discussions of race to Williams' fascination with his car, to numerous other digressional tidbits. Steinbeck, of course, employed the same style. The flow from subject to subject correlates the movement of the writers from place to place.

Besides the explicit dissection of subjects—such as racism in the armed forces, security, and black achievement—which would surface in his novels, Williams includes other interesting morsels of information. Take the following, for example, on the origins of the cakewalk:

Negro slaves, spying from behind their cabins saw the grand master's family going to church or to some other special affair. Since the slaves knew the family intimately, the majestic airs displayed on festive occasions were comical and hypocritical. At their own clandestine affairs, the slaves imitated the master and his family, grossly

17

caricaturing their way of walking, the twist of the shoulders, the swing of the arms. The slaves were caught and made to perform, before white audiences, what the master thought a purely Negro dance. When the onlookers laughed at the Negroes strutting and swinging, they were laughing at themselves. (24)

Included as well is the origin of "chitlins."

Written in a conversational prose, *This Is My Country Too* is appealing for its sincerity, its occasional straightforward journalistic accounts, its uninhibited portrayals of personal experiences. Unabashedly, Williams draws the reader into his confidence, stripping bare his own fears and hopes. At the close of the journey, Williams was as benumbed as Steinbeck but whereas the second writer found a safe haven in his New York home, the first had to refresh his soul in Africa and the Middle East. There could be symbolic implications here.

*   *   *

Covering the jackets of new books with words like "controversial" and "provocative" usually tells the prospective reader nothing about the book except that the publishers are anxious to make money. But in the case of John A. Williams' *The King God Didn't Save* (1970)[8], such words accurately forecast the nature of the book's content. A scanning of the reviews quickly confirms *The King God Didn't Save* to be the most controversial book ever written by Williams. And, why not? After all, in setting down his "Reflections on the Life and Death of Martin Luther King, Jr." (the subtitle of the book), the author harshly criticizes the public and private lives of King; and legends die hard (one need only to observe the hostility received by writers who in the last few years have attempted to demythologize the Kennedys). From his Montgomery Boycotts in 1955 to his plans for a Poor People's March, King had gained fame as the number one civil rights leader, as a Nobel Prize winner, as the savior of black people. The press, naturally, played a part in securing him his stature. Simultaneously, many people became disenchanted with his non-violent stand, his preachy oratory that seemed to end only in compromises. Yet, when he was assassinated in 1968, friend and foe alike seemed to agree

18

that he had played a vital role in the struggle for black equality. Books hurriedly went to press, recalling X and Y's experiences with King. Amidst the flurry of works that either apotheosized Reverend King or, at least, treated him with respectable leniency came Williams' account, lacking in compassion, brash, slanderous,—as some saw it—and to make things worse, Williams is a black man. How else could reviewers be expected to react? Many took the defensive and dismissed as trivia the observations of *The King God Didn't Save*. Of course, summarizing in this manner the book and the response it received oversimplifies things. A closer look must be taken at the text as well as the criticism to get a comprehensive idea of what each was saying and how it all supports a change in the racial and political views of the author.

The reviews ran two to one against Williams. Even a strong sympathizer with Williams would have to concede that his book totters organizationally. Charges of repetition and movements through time with no apparent logic are hard to oppose. What is *The King God Didn't Save* all about? Williams calls it his "reflection." The text provides further expansion. In Part One, concerning King's public life, the author admits from the beginning, "I didn't know King and, in fact, had extensive reservation about his philosophy of nonviolence" (19). In this introduction, Williams outlines his own views.

White power, avers Williams, proved the most insidious threat to King, as well it may to any man of color in the United States. King's ascendency in the mid-fifties rested on a series of events which, had they been otherwise, could have left him in obscurity. Segregationists, ironically, must be credited somewhat for the position of leadership in which King found himself. Because of his non-violent posture, King often had to watch while violence was used to insure his safety. Since a "display of power begets a display of power," he soon found himself surrounded by violence. Inevitably, he became its victim. King, like Malcolm X, posed the biggest threat to the U.S. when he extended his attacks beyond America, beyond domestic to foreign affairs.

It will not go unobserved that both Malcolm and King died as they attempted to mount programs involving not only blacks, but the oppressed of every race and kind. (78)

King's progress had been marginal, but the press inflated his gains, misleading the nation into thinking that Blacks were receiving a new equity. Also, the media created for the civil rights minister an illusion of power. He was not the first nor last to be tricked into thinking that national prominence added up to power in national affairs. So, from the beginning Martin Luther King had been deluded. Williams' assessment may be plausible, but critics take issue with the specifics of his thesis, protesting that he exaggerated facts, overstated the plight of Blacks, misread the ramifications of King's actions. Such reproof pales alongside the diatribes awaiting Part Two of the book.

In the second part of *The King God Didn't Save,* Williams concentrates on the private life of King. First, however, the author attacks Western civilization which he claims is based on money instead of morality. Directly related to this money-lust are major religions; namely, Roman Catholicism, Judaism and Protestantism. Catholic priests had sailed with slaveships to and from Africa, had given their sanction to the slave trade, had capitalized on slave labor. It appears that this Catholic power structure kept King at arm's length, often forbidding some members' involvement. Williams warns:

> Black people would do well to remember the historical participation of the Catholics in their dehumanization, and only cease to remember when Catholics have undone what they began. (124)

Certainly, the Jews do not escape blamelessly either. True, Jewish leadership had come to the aid of black people, but that was fairly recent. Too often, Jews saw Blacks as a means to commercial profit. Jewish-run stores in the ghetto and Jewish slum-lords certify for many Blacks that Jewish interests lie first with the purses and only incidentally with the persons of the ghetto. No wonder feelings of black anti-Semitism annually gain more basis in fact. And, as far as the Jews and King were concerned, Williams says, "Jewish leaders utilized King as the 'house Negro' to refute the allegations of other more militant Negroes" (141).

Protestantism finessed its way through racial biases by assigning Blacks to higher positions in its organization but denying them any real influence. Hence, behind a veneer of equality and racial fairness,

Protestants emerge as the most socially, politically and economically powerful religious sect in the States. Yet, racism caused the schism between Northern and Southern Baptists. How sad, suggests Williams, that Martin Luther King, knowing that the very religious group to which he belonged resulted from Protestant segregation, could not have avoided placing his trust in that sect. Obviously, none of the other major religious groups would have been any more reliable. And this leads back to religions being big, untrustworthy businesses. King should have turned away from organized religions altogether, Williams feels.

Like any human King had his weaknesses, and Williams outlines them. As a member of the black middle class, King was naturally a social climber for whom "the values were education, employment, and color." Because of these preoccupations, submits Williams, King found himself incapacitated when it came to empathizing with the black masses. He couldn't keep pace with their frustrations nor could he comprehend their leaning toward black power in opposition to his non-violence. Also, King seemed a poor organizer and, consequently, was called into a town usually after the groundwork had been lain. He seemed to get himself jailed at opportune times, so as to miss the more physical skirmishes. Underlying all this were his hubris and a promiscuous sex life. Unnamed interviewees support the charges. Person B recalls King gloating over his place in the polls and his childish rush to the newsstand to corroborate his popularity. Person C talks about more intimate matters.

"There were two pictures. One showed me sitting on the floor beside the bathtub in which Martin sat, naked. From the angle of the photo, it looks as though I was doing something. The other photo showed me sitting on the bed beside Martin who's laying there, nude. Now, in both cases, I was conferring with Martin in the only time available to me. Nothing, absolutely nothing took place." (190)

In the end, the indiscretions of Dr. King led to blackmail, however subtle, both by the F.B.I. and the press. He was told to quell his criticism of the F.B.I. and the government or his rompings would be made public. The same press which "reached down into the South and created King and then extolled his list of dubious victories turns out to have been a co-conspirator" (213) against him.

21

Returning to a discussion of power, the author re-emphasizes that King had been misguided:

King, believing he had power, attacked the white power structure. He did not understand that it had armed him with feather dusters . . . He was a black man and therefore always was and always would be naked of power, for he was slow — indeed unable — to perceive the manipulation of white power, and in the end white power killed him. (172,173)

Because more of Williams' time goes to emphasizing the weaknesses of Dr. Martin Luther King rather than his strengths, critics addressed themselves to the causes for this imbalance. Too often it sounds as if John A. Williams has an axe to grind in *The King God Didn't Save*. Yet, what could it be? One critic indulges in the guessing game:

There remain unanswered questions. For example, why did Williams launch his diatribe against Martin King? Perhaps he did it because he is bitter about being rebuffed in his offer to help in organizing the 1963 March . . . Or perhaps attacking Martin Luther King for being middle-class is an easy way for middle-class Negroes to acquire black credentials. I suppose the credentials are accepted, at least among Negroes traveling on similarly fraudulent papers. Perhaps, Mr. Williams just wanted to make a few dollars with a book that could be put together quickly and with a minimum of effort. Or, and I am open to this, perhaps Mr. Williams believes he has a message and is possessed by the urgent need to deliver it.[9]

Williams, himself, recently remarked as follows in response to whether he was out to get King:

I had no more against King than I've had against anybody else. I suppose from the time I was a kid and I used to see certain things go down in the black community, my feeling is anybody who puts himself into that position, no matter how they got there, vis-à-vis certain kind of leadership and who has grown up in America, knows or must have some suspicion as to how the system works. And therefore, if he's at all cognizant of the power that he wields or appears to wield for Blacks, he's an ass for getting caught up the way King got caught up.

On the other hand, one sees certain strengths he was getting to, certain things happening with the church people, for example, certain challenges that he put to Blacks who were not involved in the church. Take the junior college clique of Huey Newton, Bobby Seale and Cleaver—he put a challenge to them. A challenge was put to Stokely Carmichael. So he was a catalyst in many many areas, and as far as I'm concerned he once and for all put the lie to Western Christianity as it exists in America. That's something for black people to know and understand but it may take another century for it to really happen. So he had all of these things going for him.

I thought I made it fairly clear that he was a man subject to any of the desires or whims or whatever else appealed to most men.

I remember once having tea with Eleanor Roosevelt. I was very impressed with her; she was a very nice lady. But it was something that was not publicized. Nobody came to take pictures. It didn't appear on television. Nobody asked me what I had to say or what she had to say. Therefore, I remained, I think fortunately so, safe. Because once these things are put on film or tape and broadcast and rebroadcast, the whole "primitive" thing of having your image carried away from yourself—like not letting people take your shoelaces or your nails or a hank of hair—all that applies here in a large, if you will, electronic sense.

I looked at some of the reviews of *The King God Didn't Save*. I had to give up on them. I've read one by a black lady out in Michigan which I thought was kind of nice. She said she had been hearing a lot of stuff about the book and when she read it she was surprised because she didn't find it at all like everybody else said. But a lot of people seem to feel that I was pissed off at King because I wasn't allowed to work more on the march on Washington and other really silly assholish kinds of reasons.[10]

When *This Is My Country Too* was written, the author stood on the brink of frustration and pessimism. He knew his dedication to unveiling

23

injustices to Blacks would have an awful toll; his personal experiences reinforced this possibility. Still, he hoped and reiterated his objective [as writer] in the concluding sentences of the book: " . . . I am committed to the search for its [America's] true meaning . . ." By 1970, he had witnessed riots in the ghettoes and rebellions on campuses. He had observed the violent tactics of some law enforcers and the short-lived pacification programs of the Government. From the slight hope Williams felt in 1964, he had moved to a reluctant despair three years later. A novel in 1967 elegantly echoes his remorse, and one in 1969 does so with less elegance but more directness. So, by 1970 with the assassination of Martin Luther King, Jr., he saw a chance to accomplish two things: alert America to its congenital racism and present the life of King as a poignant example of the inability of the Black to work within the structure because he becomes the pawn of the structure.

Perhaps Williams zeal for his first goal led him to an extreme. He belabors the flaws of King to the point of arousing the suspicion of the reader. He repeats himself to make certain the impact of his message is not missed; the effect, though, is awkward. In an attempt to be fair, he acknowledges that he did not care for King's non-violent doctrine, but this causes the reader to gather he had a personal grudge against King. Most importantly, he portrays King as a *de facto* leader with peccable judgement and moral laxity. This portrayal has the following motive, verbalized in King's own speech which Williams quotes and italicizes:

"When you are written out of history as a people, when you are given no choice but to accept the majority culture, you are denied an aspect of your destiny. Ultimately you suffer a corrosion of your self-understanding and your self-respect." (136-137)

King's rise to prominence exemplifies a case in which Blacks simply assimilated the whims of the white majority. It was the press, maintains Williams, and the number of other liberal white leaders who catapulted King to fame and designated him the spokesman for black people. Meanwhile, Blacks did not question but they accepted. The weaknesses of King are irrelevant except that the white world had presented him

24

as immaculate when he was not—because it suited their purposes to have an eloquent preacher with no real power who could calm the Blacks. Then when he overstepped his bounds, steps were taken to undermine his position. Again, King's weaknesses are irrelevant except that were Blacks not denied an aspect of their own destiny—a chance to select their own leaders—a man with greater potential than King might have emerged. And even if the man had less potential, he would have been the choice of black people and they would have had a molding hand in their destiny.

It is probably too easy for one to miss the point of *The King God Didn't Save,* to ignore the author's protestation against the maneuverability of the black race. It is easier still to focus on Williams' "injustice" to King and to overlook the resident courage in his unpopular stand. Predictably, many Whites and some Blacks took shelter in their liberalism and stood aghast at the audacity of Williams.[11] But, if the book is misunderstood, Williams must share the responsibility. Like the protagonist in one of his novels, he intended to "teach down the system." Involving Martin Luther King, Jr., a man made larger than life by an influential portion of the American public, was bound to eclipse as well as distract from his intentions.

* * *

Williams published a second nonfictional book in 1970, *The Most Native of Sons,*[12] a biography of Richard Wright written for young readers. It seems more than coincidental that two of his nonfictional works were geared to the young; however, Williams disclaims any special design:

I had been asked to do these books and they were books that I thought I might enjoy doing. Of course, I don't do every book that people ask me to do, and I have mixed feelings about the young. I think that one is sort of obligated to place a great deal of faith in the ability of the young to come up with certain things if they had the information to do it with. On the other hand the young are so busy getting to some place else that they very seldom have the time to look at what's there and do the proper thing with it.

This is not really a condemnation of the young as much as it is of the system that makes it so that they don't take advantage of the tools that are available.[13]

Nonetheless, *The Most Native of Sons* like *Africa: Her History, Lands and People* educates its readers whatever the age. The first section covers much of the material as Wright's autobiography, *Black Boy*. It lacks the force and emotion of the autobiography but competition was not the purpose. Rather, Williams' intent was to present a short, concise, accurate account of Wright's life, and this he did—knowingly omitting details which might have been incorporated in a more exhaustive study.

Section Two records Wright's escape from the South to Chicago. There, too, he would be disillusioned. True, he need worry less about entering restaurants through sidedoors or about getting a job, but discrimination still prevailed. Blacks were regarded as cheap labor and menial jobs were reserved for them. Getting employment in the civil service, notably the Post Office department, represented the least shaky hope of job security.

In the midst of a national depression Communist organizations gained strength, attacking capitalism and deifying the proletariat. Wright felt Communism contained the salvation for black people, and in 1934 he joined the John Reed Club. Ten years after, he would quit the Party, convinced of its indifference to Blacks. Subsequently, he would become an expatriate writer in Europe. *The Most Native of Sons* follows Wright until his death in 1960.

The ultimate disaffection of white and black readers, who had applauded *Native Son*, with the later works of the author bordered on the tragic. Rather than deal with the unflattering accusations he made about racism in America, many rationalized that he was out of touch with America and overstated conditions here. Such reactions pained Wright but he never relented, never compromised what he saw as the truth for the popularity of the lie.

It seems fitting that Williams would have written this short work on Richard Wright. Many similarities can be found between the two. In general, they both dedicated themselves to exposing racial injustice. One novel by Williams depicts the struggle of a black family, reminiscent somewhat of *Native Son*. Another has a character who seems partly modeled on Wright. It is entirely possible that whatever likeness to Wright found in Williams may be attributed to their having shared the black experience in America. But if only because of this common background, the latter writer is able to infuse his work with an empathy that elevates *The Most Native of Sons* from just another kid's book to a sincere treatment of a fellow soldier, respected for never abandoning the fight.

It is also significant that Williams should write on both Martin Luther King, Jr. and Richard Wright. Yet, his handling of the two differs widely. Wright is portrayed as the positive antithesis to King. Although both had been victims of an instant-popularity syndrome, they had reacted differently. King thrived in his fame; Wright questioned it.

While being nationally applauded for *Native Son,* Wright wondered, according to Williams, "Could these benefits be the manner in which the system hoped to blind the eyesight, stop up his ears, soften his words" (73)? Whereas King had a middle-class background, Wright had first-hand knowledge of poverty and deprivation. King's education came formally in universities; Wright had to teach himself. Wright could understand why he sometimes stirred harsh criticism from Blacks, but King could not immediately comprehend why other Blacks would espouse black power, a tactic contrasting with his. And, whereas Wright never abandoned efforts to write about the institutional racism in America, there were times when King seemed to be selling out the civil rights movements for his own prestige. On the one hand, Williams says about Wright's novel *Savage Holiday:*

Through a white character, then, Richard was trying to symbolize once again what it was like for black men in America. They were trapped, scampering here and there looking for an exit from their dilemma. On another level Richard was dealing with the limiting concepts of white western society and how they could, in the end, lead to frustration and death, regardless of the position one had in that society. (95)

On the other hand, Williams claims that King was unable "to perceive the manipulation of white power . . ."

Observing how Williams treats Richard Wright in *The Most Native of Sons* might lead to inferences on what types of goals Williams has set for himself as writer and a person. What cannot go unnoticed is Wright's devotion to history. "Few American writers," says Williams, "applied history to their work as Richard did" (134). Wright might very well have been one of the catalysts for Williams' religious usage of history in his writings.

*   *   *

Presumably there comes a point for every writer when he looks over his shoulder at his literary efforts throughout the years. *Flashbacks*[14] (1973), while not being such a broad assessment, nevertheless provides a retrospective glance at Williams' ideological growth as reflected in his articles. The full title of the book adequately describes its contents: *Flashbacks: A Twenty-Year Diary of Article Writing*. Arranged in three sections, the most recent work of the author spans a variety of topics in articles, many of which were previously unpublished.

Section One, "Topicalities," has articles on the New York State Fair, Israel, South Africa, the black family, black middle class and church. "The Negro Middle Class" defuses the impression that the more well-to-do Blacks are unconcerned about black problems. Rather unsettling, it reminds one of the great likelihood that the same middle class, often dismissed as Uncle Toms, may well be the locus for the beginning of violent black/white confrontation. The idea is elaborated and enacted fictionally in a 1969 novel.

Personalities comprise the second section. Charlie Parker, Dick Gregory, Marcus Garvey, Malcolm X are some of the noted personages discussed. Williams includes here "Chester Himes—My Man Himes," an interview with the writer of *Cast the First Stone, The Third Generation,* and numerous other fictions. This interview offers a rare glimpse of a meeting of two literary giants exchanging views on the arts and on black life. (The article appears initially in *Amistad 1,* a journal edited by Williams and Charles F. Harris.) Despite suppressing his opinions in deference to Himes', Williams still reveals not just his skill as an interrogator but his admiration for a writer, who like himself, had endured difficult times.

Section Three, entitled "Personals," is the most moving and appealing part of the book. For it is here that the reader gains immense insight into Williams the man. "We Regret to Inform You That" registers details of an unfortunate incident with the Academy that awards the Prix de Rome for writing. (This article can be found in its entirety in an upcoming chapter of this study.) "A Pessimistic Postscript" records the author's assessment of the black civil rights movement in 1967; "Time and Tide: The Roots of Black Awareness" furthers this subject. The gem of the section is "Career by Accident." With unexpected honesty, Williams bares his soul about how he became a writer, never shying away from personal or private revelations. One can hardly leave this article uninspired or nonappreciative.

What adds tremendously to *Flashbacks* are the brief introductory remarks to each article which places the piece in context. These introductions document the ups and downs the writer underwent, and he has his day in court against publishers, for one. In a related vein he recently remarked that

The lack of receipt of literary prizes in this country by black authors reinforces the idea that Black Literature is separate and distinct from American Literature. Because when white writers receive these prizes—on the back of a book jacket you notice that so and so is a Guggenheim fellow and so on—it tends to improve their status, their figures as writers. When Blacks don't get them, that means in effect that they are not good writers. This in turn reinforces the pay schedule—that's the proletarian pay schedule. There is white money and there is black money for books that are produced by the two racial groups. And publishers know it, white writers know it and black writers know it. There is very little effort on the part of white writers—with the exception of the Authors Guild which doesn't really operate in that area just yet—to equalize this ratio. Many black writers suspect it, but they don't suspect how deep down it goes, and therefore they're not in a position to really act on it. We're all in a situation of just being damn happy we have a book contract because the signing of a book contract is supposed to elevate us to some mythical realm of heroism or Valhalla or what have you.

Some people talk about renegade Blacks who write a book and get rich and go off and leave the brothers and sisters. That is exactly the kind of perspective that most black people have about writers. The hard fact is that we don't, for reasons that I've just specified. I think black publishers have not grown up to the extent where they have the money, the distribution or anything else that could remotely compare to the bankroll that white publishers have. To that extent they remind me of weekly newspaper publishers that I used to know: they expect you to work for nothing, they expect you to work hard and to work well and to understand why it is they don't have the money to pay you, even though they're dealing in the white man's contract which says that you're supposed to be paid at certain specific times. But, black publishers because of the racist situation among white publishers and the whole literary world will take undue advantage of black writers who choose to publish with them.[15]

Sometimes, the tone of the book is bitter; sometimes it is indifferent, sometimes elated, sometimes hostile. But whatever the tone, a sincerity emerges that rises beyond reproach. Perhaps shocking to many is Williams lack of timidity in mentioning names, places and dates. As a cross-section of his short nonfiction, *Flashbacks* has a wealth of ideas matched by no other book of the author. For this reason, it serves as the most comprehensive supplement to the fiction.

*　　*　　*

Anyone who reads the nonfiction of Williams then turns to the novels does so with a distinct advantage. He brings a familiarity with the themes that are important to the author. Detecting undercurrent themes or autobiographical data or reasons for emphasis on a particular topic at a particular time becomes a simpler accomplishment. The reader with this broader consciousness of what is going on can all the better appreciate the subtleties of the works. Conversely, if one reads the fiction first and the nonfiction second, one would certainly gain an education and amplification of the former from the latter. The point is that whereas for some writers their factual and fictional works may be totally unrelated, the opposite is exactly the case for Williams. As a consequence, any student of his novels will find the nonfictional books indispensable tools.

Notes To Chapter One

1. John A. Williams, *Africa: Her History, Lands and People* (New York: Cooper Square, 1963). Subsequent references will be to the 1969 edition.
2. "Williams Publishes History of Africa," *World*, 24 March 1964.
3. Harry J. Anslinger and J. Dennis Gregory, *The Protectors* (New York: Farrar, Straus & Co., 1964).
4. A note in the John A. Williams Collection in the George Arents Research Library for Special Collections at Syracuse University.
5. From an interview with John A. Williams on September 28, 1973.
6. *Ibid.*
7. Williams, *This Is My Country Too* (New York: New American Library, 1965). Subsequent references will be to the 1966 Signet edition.
8. _____, *The King God Didn't Save* (New York: Coward-McCann, Inc., 1970). Subsequent references will be to this edition.
9. Richard J. Neuhaus, "Martin Luther King's Second Assasination," *New York Review of Books*, 8 October 1970, p. 49.
10. From September 28, 1973 interview.
11. Charles Dollen, for one, accused Williams of black racism in *Best Sellers*, September 1970, p. 208.
12. Williams, *The Most Native of Sons* (New York: Doubleday & Co., 1970).
13. From September 28, 1973 interview.
14. Williams, *Flashbacks* (New York: Doubleday, 1973).
15. From September 28, 1973 interview.

Two

Tainted Chicken: The Angry Ones

I spent a lot of time thinking and starving to death. I think at that
time I was drawing $36.00 a week from unemployment. Greg and
Dennis came down once, and I had this chicken that seemed to
be a little tainted—I wasn't sure. But I had to face the big decision
whether I was to give these guys this chicken that I believed to
be tainted or really show myself for what I was, which was absolutely
penniless; I didn't have another quarter. What I did was, I was
going to fry the chicken, but, I decided to boil it. I boiled it and
boiled it. I boiled that son of a bitch to death. Until, if there was
a taint left in it, it couldn't have lived. So we had boiled chicken
and some vegetables. I don't think they ever knew about it.

This vignette captures the embarrassment of a man barely able to feed
himself much less his two sons. Amidst such hard times, John A.Williams
would see a story he had written at the age of thirty become his first
published novel at the age of thirty-five. *The Angry Ones* (1960)[1] is
the story of Stephen Hill, a black public relations man, who faces
the ordeal of maintaining dignity and finding employment in New York
City. Newly arrived from Los Angeles, he descends on Manhattan
with the exuberance of a child, feeling quite certain that the right job
awaits him somewhere. It takes but a rejection or two to stunt his
enthusiasm, to revive memories of his near-fatal depression in Los
Angeles where he had spent more than six months without getting
acceptable work. He thinks, too, of his family's faith in education,
of his being "the first to receive the skin with the college stamp on
it" (6), and of the irony that an educated Black faces a double burden,
since his academic exposure has made him aware of what rights there

are for man, of the infinite possibilities that exist—but not for him. How Steve Hill confronts this harsh reality is the focus of the novel. *The Angry Ones* is largely autobiographical. It documents the hard times Williams had faced when he settled in New York in the mid-fifties. He had worked for a vanity publishing house and knew first-hand the discrimination a Black encountered in the advertising and publicity fields at that time. Perhaps, feeling that his own experiences were tragic enough, he wrote on those rather than construct a totally imagined world. In most of his fiction Williams would never wander far from actual facts and experiences with which he was closely familiar.

So Steve Hill, like Williams, is an educated Black who must face up to being black and all that it implied in the late fifties. Plotwise, the novel appears to be but another formula protest novel. Its main character encounters racial discrimination rebelliously and the narrator passes up no opportunity to intrude with didactic commentary against racism. A close examination of the text, however, reveals subtle treatment of themes which elevate the book from pure formula fiction.

The bigoted white boss and the black well-intentioned employee is an example of a conflict which might be found in any protest novel. And in *The Angry Ones,* Steve Hill is placed opposite Rollie Culver, his white boss. But, an extra dimension is added. Culver is a calculating homosexual. Besides that, he is a shrewd businessman. He knows that no matter how good Steve is, his job opportunities are limited because of his black skin. Hence, he sees Steve as cheap labor and refuses to increase his salary unless Steve is willing to surrender himself to him. The white homosexual employer or patron would become a recurring figure in Williams' fiction. Not only does a Steve Hill have to submit to the racial slights of the white business world, but he also has to submit to Rollie Culver's amorous overtures. It is as if Williams were saying that the Black too often has to give over his manhood physically as well as psychologically to survive in the white world. Other black writers had long emphasized this psychological surrender; but not many confronted the physical one.

Instead of having Steve commit a brutal act at some point in the novel, Williams shows tremendous insight on the effect of black violence on some whites: When Rollie tries to seduce Steve, Steve hits him; then notices that ''he kind of smiled with his eyes . . . I wondered if he liked that sort of thing" (70). Later, Steve's suspicion would be confirmed. About to strike Rollie again, he notes that Rollie "had been ready to stand there and feed on my violence" (182). Then, he resolves:

Let them shake and expect the violence they deserve, but never give it to them . . . because they derive strength from it, as Rollie wanted strength from me now. But I wasn't going to give it to him. (182)

The observation that some Whites take masochistic delight in black violence or maybe assuage some guilt because of this type of reaction indicates that Williams was doing more than just writing about black retaliation. He was examining how it might be received and how it might help to soothe those same people the Blacks may be trying to hurt. Other writers would return to this idea as the study of racism increased during the sixties and seventies.[2]

In protest fiction, it would be expected that somewhere would enter the neurotic white woman who joins up with the black protagonist, usually bringing more problems than she solves. Lois, in *The Angry Ones,* fits this description. Yet, Williams carries his study further. He acknowledges that white/black romantic involvements need not be and are not so limited in real life. It is possible that both individuals could be quite sane and honestly in love with each other.[3] It is also possible that both individuals could be exploiting each other; and such is the case with Steve and Lois. On the one hand Lois is a mixed-up girl who uses Steve as a means of rebelling against her puritanical parents. On the other hand, Williams emphasizes, Steve uses Lois as his buffer against the daily horrors at work or on the streets. After maliciously asking Lois to marry him, Steve mercilessly hits her with his assessment of their relationship.

"You used me as a tool against your parents—against your mother. You wanted to get even with her, . . . I used you too, baby. Oh, hell, I'm not clean in this. You had many faces, Lois, and I realize now I hated every white one of them. Nearly every time I called you, it had been a bad day for me, and I had to get back, if not at them directly, at you, and that worked out fine. It kept me from going nuts . . . What is it you can't accept, Lois—that Negroes can think and feel and want revenge? . . . You wanted revenge for the way folks treated you. I wanted revenge for the way people treated me. We're even. Retaliation all around." (165)

With the cards on the table, their relationship ends. Like many a black and white couple under the relentless pressures from the outside, they survive as long as the symbiotic union remains an unspoken one; once its nature is acknowledged, it becomes difficult to continue the charade.

No doubt, Williams' interest in Lois and Steve, a white woman and black man, can be traced to his years in Syracuse, New York, where he claims interracial romances had not been unique. Further, his years between marriages were spent dating black and white women. Nevertheless, this interest in the black man/white woman relationship seems an important one for him and one to which he returns in his fiction.[4]

Other cases in which Williams surpasses the peripheral study of race which may be found in a protest novel can be illustrated in his handling of certain themes. For instance, black pride is an important ingredient for the Black who wants to forge ahead but maintain dignity and integrity. But in *The Angry Ones,* Williams demonstrates the limitations of racial pride. Obie Robertson, journalist friend of Steve's, finds himself jobless. He determines not to compromise by taking just any job that comes along. While his pride soars, he sinks further into poverty and despair. At one point in his despondency, he ponders his plight as a black man refusing to accept the harshness of racism:

There's got to be a flaw in me . . . It can't be the thing, it's got to be me . . . But I . . . can't believe discrimination can be *this* horrible . . . No, I can't believe it. I've got a flaw and I've got to work it out." (160)

He poses the age-old question whether Blacks are mostly paranoids attributing every ill to race prejudice or genuinely victims because of race.[5] Ultimately he concludes that the prejudice is to be blamed, not him, and he commits suicide. Williams is not denouncing black pride but he is saying that pride alone rarely feeds a hungry mouth or supplies a job. In this sense, Obie contrasts sharply with Steve. Steve also has pride, but he is willing to scheme, to connive, to accept, temporarily, less than he deserves in order to survive. What Williams bluntly implies is that if survival is the objective one may very well have to do what Steve did; and although one's dignity may not be totally intact, it need not be completely shattered either. If martyrdom is the objective, one may follow Obie's path and trust that suicide would be no stigma to one's honor.

Although Steve returns to his childhood girlfriend at the close of *The Angry Ones,* Williams does not suggest that all will go well for him now that he has turned to a woman his own color. The author's portrayal of Grace enables him to probe another subject—security. Steve and Grace have conflicting ideas on security. As Steve sees it, a man must have his dreams. "You're walking around dead if you don't dream" (5), and sometimes dreams can be more important than life itself. So when a man considers a mate, he wants someone who will share his dreams. To Grace he says, "You wouldn't fight or dream with me" (145). As Grace sees it, a black man should accept his pigmentation and not feel a constant need to fight. Should Steve take a job as a social worker with the civil service (a symbol of security), all could be so much better. Having the stability of home, family, and means to support them are all-important to her. Steve agrees with their importance, but insists on having the job he wants, a job which would testify to his worth and dignity. He had seen how

the fierce desire for security was born in her. And it grew. It became a monster which consumed the love we had for each other as if it had never existed. (37)

Marrying Grace on her terms might well be a defeat since it would mean recasting his whole life's aim. Finally, Grace yields. Nevertheless, she does have her type of security in her late husband's untouched insurance money.

In *This Is My Country Too* Williams had more to say about that illusive ideal called security:

You are damned if you have it, and goddamned if you don't. Big house, two cars, a yard, television, a savings account. Good, good, but at what expense? Oh, this is not true only of my friend a black instructor in the South, it is true of most Americans who almost invariably confuse security with status. And they saddle themselves through brief lifetimes with jobs and bosses they don't like, associating with people they detest or even hate, just for security and/or status. (74-75)

The reason Williams attacks security so vociferously and repeatedly throughout his works is because an important part of his life had been altered because of disagreements over security. He was a caseworker for Onondaga County Department of Welfare in Syracuse, and he became disillusioned for reasons echoed by Steve: " 'I couldn't be a social worker, man. I couldn't stand anyone else's misery. I got enough of my own' " (105). Unable to accept the eight-to-five tradition, the saving to buy house, car and fashionable clothes, Williams found his first marriage floundering. On the other hand, his wife was more practical. She wanted to know how the family would survive if he became suddenly ill; she wanted him to be able to provide more finances than his writing was obtaining. Of course, there were other problems as well. With two children and six years of married life behind him, he set out in 1952 to pursue his writing career and to leave job security behind to those who would have them. His whole lifestyle became a protest, then, against considering the attainment of the American dream as the ultimate satisfaction, and he never misses a chance to criticize security and status, handmaidens of the American dream, in his works.

To prevent *The Angry Ones* from being overly one-sided, the author introduces white characters who affirm that Blacks have no monopoly on suffering. These characters give a balance to the story not often found in protest novels which tend to depict Blacks as the sole recipients of abuse. Even though this exaggeration may be understandable, such works tend to lose credibility because of their incessant complaining and self-righteous tone. Williams escapes this effect by the inclusion of Lint, Bobbie and Crispus.

Lint and Steve Hill have been schoolmates; however Lint's being white guaranteed him an easier path to success. Still, he has his problems. He constantly competes with his wife, Bobbie, who aspires to be an actress. To have her succeed before he does would be mortifying.

Further, he has fits of jealousy. So with Lint trying to undermine any achievement of Bobbie's, he finds himself making little headway of his own. And, with Bobbie turning to outside lovers to compensate for her marital turmoil, the couple's problems are compounded. Lint finds a good excuse for dragging Steve into the mire when he sees Lois, who looks like Bobbie, going into Steve's apartment. In fact, even before this incident, he had always wondered how much Bobbie and Steve were attracted to each other. His insecurity can undoubtedly be traced to the sexual myth that a black man desires with every fibre in his body to seduce a white woman and she, in turn, can little help a fascination for the brute sexuality he exudes.[6] No wonder Lint wants to castrate Steve.

Crispus is a white Southerner who represents to Steve "the epitome of Crackerhood." Like Lint and Bobbie, Crispus has difficulties in spite of his white skin. Rollie exploits him by taking his money in return for shaky hopes of a best seller. His money gone and illusions of being a famous author shattered, Crispus in his rage and hurt tries to kill Rollie. Regardless of an instinctive dislike for Crispus, Steve identifies with him somewhat, for they are both dreamers and both are victims of the business world.

Williams touches on a subject in *The Angry Ones* which would be much expanded in later novels, particularly *Sissie*. The subject is guilt. At one point, Steve thinks that "as opportunities for Negroes appeared on the surface to be getting better, they would at the same time become subtly worse for some segments" (20). This increased opportunity for a few Blacks at the expense of a lack of opportunity for the black masses could only lead to guilt feelings in those successful Blacks who are sensitive about the progress of their race as a whole. Not enough exploration into the guilt of the successful few had been done by social critics. Williams would make it his business to expose this guilt.

All in all, *The Angry Ones* fits the mode of the protest novel, but more importantly, it surpasses that mode in its handling of theme and character. A last example of this is the conclusion, which is bleak yet hopeful. Rather than have his protagonist totally subdued by his maltreatment, Williams has him survive in spite of it. Steve is more convinced than ever that he must continue to fight. And in the sense that the struggle is not won, the novel ends bleakly. But in the sense that he resolves to do the best he can and looks forward to the next generation's having a more equitable existence, the novel closes on a note of hope. Still, the shakiness of this hope in the novel is a reflection of Williams' view of real life.

The history of *The Angry Ones* is interesting in itself. John A. Williams had completed two novels in 1955 and 1958, *One For New York* and *The Cool Ones,* respectively (the former was retitled *The Angry Ones).* Between 1955 and 1960, he sent one, then both manuscripts all over New York in search of a publisher. *The Cool Ones* remains unpublished.[7]

One For New York differed somewhat from the final version of *The Angry Ones.* In one version, Williams begins with Steve's phoning a clinic to arrange an appointment with a psychiatrist. The secretary tells him he'll have to make an appointment for the next day. Totally frustrated, he slams the phone down and takes an overdose of sleeping pills. In another manuscript, a chapter occurs in Los Angeles; Steve's younger borther, Dave, is introduced and is seen encouraging Steve about job prospects. This contrasts with the final text in which Dave is introduced through flashbacks but never really comes alive. And, although Steve does try killing himself with an overdose, the call to the doctor is omitted. There were approximately five drafts of *One For New York;* obviously, it received endless reworking. Moreover, the author's patience must have been sorely taxed as rejections came repeatedly. Each time he sent the novel to another company, his hopes would rise. Sooner or later the manuscripts returned with apologies, and sometimes, with sincere criticism. Some publishers which refused *One For New York* were Ballantine Books, Inc., Appleton-Century-Crofts, Inc., The Dial Press Inc., The Viking Press Inc., The Bobbs Merrill Company Inc., Gold Medal Books, and David McKay Company Inc. The comments from the David McKay Company illustrate a rare effort to be helpful:

The problems which Steve Hill faces in ONE FOR NEW YORK are those of modern man PLUS.—there is the problem of man finding himself, of establishing an identity, and the additional problem faced by the negro, who has to battle with himself *and* society. A great deal has been written and said about these difficulties, and to present them in a new and forceful light is a hard task. A certain amount of sympathy for the struggling one on the part of the reader is automatic, but to really move him and make him think and reevaluate there must be more depth, and more importance than we have here. The worst examples of terrible things which befall the hero are not really so very bad. Being mocked on the street by a gang of hoodlums is no unusual experience, and those experiences which are truly demoralising—such as the real difficulties of finding a job and a place to live—are not projected with the force they should have. These passages ought to be reworked so that the situations which are stated become situations which are felt. It is necessary to build a stronger picture of Steve trudging, struggling, constantly faced by blank walls, perhaps going hungry, or at least having difficulty in keeping up his appearance. A bit more desperation must come across, or his suicidal thoughts are baseless. The literature which came out of the depression sets some wonderful examples of struggle amidst near hopelessness. Also, the job which Steve finally gets does not sound bad enough, or his boss low enough to justify his complete disgust. If the firm were really fly-by-night, and the boss an almost complete crook, then the punch in the nose finale would be more justified. However, even without that last punch, and keeping the job and boss just as they are Steve's feeling of the uselessness and utter mediocrity of his job must come across more strongly. The author's problem here, as in the entire work, is one of reworking for strength. There is no doubt that the author feels the hero's plight deeply, but in setting it down formally, the edge seems to have worn off. There ought, I feel, to be more physical description of the people who reject him, and more words from them. The specific examples of rejection should be stronger—the scenes with the hoodlums uglier—more menacing. If perhaps the hoodlum scene started with a semi-nasty conversation in a bar in which one tough taunted Steve, another began to force his attentions on Lois, and others joined them and followed Steve and Lois when they left the bar there would be a sense of real danger. As it is, the New Yorker who has himself been followed and taunted finds it difficult to understand the terror and anger and unbelief of the victims in this case. All the "show-downs" here need to be built up to more.

The relationships between Steve and the girls he meets are rather unclear. What are his actual feelings for Grace, for Lois? Does he feel real love for Lois? Could he if he loves Grace? Does he love Grace? His actions are described, but the state of his emotions left in doubt. He is not a character who moves through his life in a dream-like and unemotional state—his suicide attempt and the anguish which precedes it testify to that, so we must know more about how he feels towards the people in his life. He tells certain things to Lois, but in the form of analysis of past action, and here the reader is left out of the scene.

Lastly—I wonder about the function of the "cool" narration. The hero is able to speak jazz and English, and in fact, uses English at his job, and presumably did in school, but speaks modern jazz talk with his friends. He is not, as is Jack Kerouak, all of a piece with his living speech and writing speech. The character is not a member of the beat, and his aims are in the world of conformity, or at least of organized society. Yet the narration is "cool." Since this book is aimed at the general public, which doesn't dig the lingo, and since the hero is attempting to make his life in the areas in which the general public lives, he ought to speak the public language, with, of course, the subtleties of a writer. It is quite natural for Steve to speak in this fashion with some of his friends, but must he address the reader thus?[8]

Of course, all responses were not so meticulous; many of the other companies dismissed the book as too bitter, not worth the while, or too abusive to Whites. A few of the rejection notes are a study in prejudice. In 1960 Williams obtained his break, and not a moment too soon either: he had intended to abandon writing had his bad luck continued. Ace Books, Inc. released *The Angry Ones* (they changed the title for commercial reasons) in a cheap paper edition (for thirty-five cents, what could one expect—even in 1960?). Still, John A. Williams was not totally launched as a writer. His book got buried on obscure bookracks. One year afterwards, when his second novel reached the public, not half of the reviewers knew that he had written *The Angry Ones*. Only a Pocket Book edition printed in 1970 rescued it from oblivion.

One may criticize the action, characterization and autobiographical data in *The Angry Ones*. The David McKay Company had complained that nothing really terrible occurred to Steve Hill. In its final form the book still falls prey to this complaint. One explanation is that the book is dated, and what might seem an expression of anger in the novel is mild in comparison to the militancy of some Blacks today. Another explanation may be that Williams wanted to show that Blacks need not have colossal tragedies to become frustrated and to feel discrimination. The hurt a man feels for being refused housing because of his color may readily weigh equally with the hurt he might experience if he were physically attacked. In a sense, then, no racial slight can be considered minor.

A weakness in the novel is the many stock characters. For example, Lois is the confused White motivated by revenge; Grace is the security seeker, Bobbie the exploiter, Obie the oppressed Black, Lint and Bobbie the typical, insecure, middle-class Whites. Each character stays within his mold, which tends to abort any attempts at surprise. Once the reader realizes in what niche an individual belongs, building suspense around him becomes a futile endeavor.

A question arises about the extensive inclusion of autobiographical data. After all, besides the main plot of *The Angry Ones,* numerous other items were lifted directly from the author's life; such as the job hunt in New York City, the distressing times in Los Angeles. Also, Steve's parents and brother in the novel are modeled on Williams' family. This autobiographical emphasis continues in other fiction. As suggested earlier, Williams' main reason for remaining close to his immediate experiences are that they are tragic enough; consequently, there is little need to turn elsewhere. Undeniably, though, he does use the imaginative process to shape his materials and give them a form which can convey his ideas sometimes with subtlety, sometimes with poignance. In other words, the admixture of fiction and fact (particularly well-known facts) by Williams furnishes his novels with an historical realism which adds more authenticity to the non-factual elements. Later novels would illustrate this effect more clearly.

43

If *The Angry Ones,* in spite of weaknesses, does have strengths which take it beyond the bounds of the protest novel, why was its initial reception so poor? An answer may be conjectural though revealing. To begin with, *The Angry Ones* was a poorly distributed paperback. Also, it appeared during a period when James Baldwin held the title of novelist-spokesman for Blacks. Williams' book, like any other black fiction of the time, might have found itself being measured according to Baldwin's. Since the country saw no need for additional black, so-called protest, novelists—particularly one that seemed not as good as Baldwin—books like *The Angry Ones* perished. Further, critics and reviewers were already convincing their readers that America had had enough protest writings from Blacks. Although Baldwin would still be tolerated, if not praised, other Blacks should be more creative (this becomes ludicrous in the light of Baldwin's *Giovanni's Room,* 1956, when some said Baldwin should return to the race question). So, a straightforward book detailing a black man's plight was a bore. As happens from time to time, the critics, perhaps inadvertently, commited an inhumane act as they desensitized the reading public to a real human suffering which knows no season. Needless to say, the critics do not deserve full blame. The Civil Rights Movement was gaining in press coverage. More of white America had to come to terms with the "other America." No doubt, many white Americans, imposed on enough by the black struggle on television, radio and in the newspapers, had no special appetite for more in their leisure reading. In other times (the last five years, for example), books less well-written than *The Angry Ones* have been rushed to the press simply *because* they were by Blacks. It is unfortunate that the cries, writings, and hopes of a people must depend on fads, must wait until they become fashionable before receiving attention. *The Angry Ones* was re-issued in 1970, and although many bought the book because they had read other works by John A. Williams, undoubtedly as many bought it because the jacket includes the words "angry" and "Negro writer." With his second novel, Williams would have greater success.

Notes To Chapter Two

1. John A. Williams, *The Angry Ones* (New York: Ace Books, 1960). All subsequent references will be to the 1970 Pocket Books edition.
2. Social critic Albert Murray elaborates Williams' observations ten years later in *The Omni-Americans* (New York: Outerbridge & Dienstfrey, 1970), p. 96. : . . . White integrationists are far more likely to condemn and reject their clean-cut, professionally competent black neighbors for not being black enough than to congratulate or simply accept them for not being problems. "Man," said one middle-aged black resident of Westchester County, a man who has spent his whole life working for better Negro education, job opportunities, and civil rights, "you go to one of those parties and fail to show the proper enthusiasm for Malcolm, Rap, and Cleaver, and then some ofay millionaire and his wife will call you an Uncle Tom to your face! And you know who will back them up? Almost every establishment editor present. Man, it's getting so that if you don't go in there pissing and moaning and making threats, they'll call you a moderate and drop your butt fifty times faster than Malcolm ever would. You got to cuss them out, or you're out of it, buddy. But damn, man, the minute you sound off, you realize that they've tricked you into scat singing buck dancing for them; because there they are, all crowding around, like watching you masturbate, like they are ready to clap their hands and yell, 'Go, man, go. Get hot, Man.' But Goddamnit, you know what they really want you to be? 'A blind man with a guitar!' "
3. See *Night Song* in which Williams labors to impress the reader that Keel and Della have a very wholesome relationship devoid of the stereotypical neuroses which are expected to accompany black and white romances. Max and Margrit in *The Man Who Cried I Am* fall into a pattern similar to Keel and Della's relationship.
4. It is tempting to relate Williams' treatment in his fiction of black man/white woman relationships not only to his own experiences in that area but to his eventually marrying a white woman (his second wife). However, such correlation seems, at most, tenuous and hazardous.
5. Williams lampoons the question of black paranoia in an interchange between Ralph Joplin, Jr. and his psychiatrist in *Sissie*.
6. See Sterling Brown's explanation of The Brute Negro in "Negro Character as Seen by White Authors" in *Dark Symphony,* eds. James A. Emanuel and Theodore L. Gross (New York: The Free Press, 1968), pp. 139-171. Brown quotes from *The Negro: The Southerner's Problem* by Thomas Nelson Page who records that "The Negro's passion, always his controlling force, is now, since the new teaching, for the white woman."
7. *The Cool Ones* traces the lives and loves, the rise and fall of three Blacks as schoolmates and as servicemen. A great part of the novel follows their lives during the Korean War. As a whole the story is weak because the action rarely transcends the mundane and its writing lacks the force which might have salvaged whatever was wanting in depth. *The Cool Ones* seems to indicate that a combat setting was one which Williams had not handled to his satisfaction; probably because he had experienced racial injustice during his stint in the navy and could not rest until he exposed these injustices in fiction or nonfiction. Another observation about the unpublished novel is that it contains characters similar to those that would appear in later fiction. For

example, the mother of Johnny Court, one of the protagonists, is obviously a forerunner of Sissie Joplin of *Sissie*.

8. This critique from the David McKay Company is in the John A. Williams Collection in the George Arents Research Library for Special Collections at Syracuse University.

Three

No Sambo Smiles: Night Song

Intending a tribute to the late jazz musician Charlie Parker, John
A. Williams and Robert George Reisner began writing *Bird,* the life
of Parker, in 1959. After Reisner's departure, Williams continued solo
for a while before quitting. But what he completed was eventually
to evolve into his second novel *Night Song* (1961).[1] Reviewers were
quick to explain the parallels of the novel to real life. Some even
noticed a trend:

> Jazz novels comprise a whole sub-genre in American fiction. Dorothy
> Baker may or may not have started it all with *Young Man With
> a Horn,* her fictionalized account of the temptations and excesses
> of cornetist Bix Beiderbecke. Each year a new one is added to the
> list. The best of them have been Shelby Foote's short novel, *Ride
> Out,* and John Clellon Holmes' *The Horn.* The latest (at this
> writing) is Ross Russell's *The Sound.* Most follow the pattern
> set by Dorothy Baker and concentrate on a single, legend-
> in-his-own-time character, borrowing heavily on actual events, per-
> sonalities and conversations. *The Horn* presented a portrait of tenor
> saxophonist Lester Young, somewhat altered, and generally more
> flattering than he may have deserved. *Night Song* has as its pivotal
> figure a thinly disguised Charlie "Yardbird" Parker—"Bird" for
> short.[2]

One writer compared *Night Song* to Ross Russell's *The Sound:*

> One of its [*Night Song's*] principal characters, Richie (Eagle) Stokes,
> is as clearly based on Charlie Parker, as was Red Travers of the
> Russell book.

47

All the other main links in the plot are the same, too: the New York setting, the white cat who doesn't quite fit the scene, the interracial romance, the racial conflict, the quest for refuge through Mohammedanism, the heroin-shooting, and the Bird-man's eventual fate.[3]

Another reviewer generously reports:

> Though the ghost of Charles Parker and his omnipotent horn haunt *Night Song*—as almost every novel on jazz since the great man died—the book is head and shoulders above the others, a real gem.[4]

The preceding critiques should confirm the suspicion that Williams was aiming at a fictional characterization of Charlie Parker as Richie (Eagle) Stokes. Nonetheless, *Night Song* progresses far beyond this parallel. There is, of course, the story of Eagle whose existential philosophy was acquired not through any study of great thinkers but through having very little choice. Then, there is Hillary whom Eagle rescues, and Keel, Eagle's "guardian angel," and Della, the girl for whom Keel and Hillary vie. How the lives of these four intermesh makes for a novel so intriguing as to merit a National Institute of Arts and Letters grant for its author.

David Hillary, an English instructor and a member of a "deep-rooted, native American" Protestant family, typifies the White who cannot escape sharing the prejudices his race has against Blacks. Yet, Hillary rises beyond a mere type to a character who has his own idiosyncrasies, strengths and limitations. Blaming himself for the accidental death of his wife, he seeks solace in alcohol. He presents a seedy image when he attempts to pawn his five hundred dollar wedding band. It is in this pawnshop that he meets Eagle who, sensing Hillary's desperation, follows him out of the store. Even in his drunken stupor, Hillary can react only with fear to a black man following him. However, his visions of being assaulted vanish when he recognizes Eagle as the famed jazz saxophonist. While still in the company of Eagle, the bereaved Hillary loses consciousness, then awakens in a room off from Keel's nightclub. Keel had salvaged him only because of Eagle's insistence. Soon, Hillary sees Della and notes her affection for Keel: a white woman in love with a black man. Automatically searching her face, Hillary could not find what he assumed had to be there in cases like this.

There was no sign of any neurotic defiance hidden in her eyes, nothing to suggest that she harbored any deep, self-hatred for this need to see Keel. (23)

Williams observes how typical the former English instructor's suspicions were in another book:

On the whole the white American male is a peculiar creature. He tends to have a proprietary interest in any white female seen with a Negro male. (*This is My Country Too,* p. 128.)

Disappointed at finding no neuroses which would explain away Della's involvement with Keel, Hillary deludes himself into thinking that he's infatuated with her. His lust for Della becomes clear as he substitutes her in his mind for a loathsome prostitute with whom he has sex.

Upon encountering another white woman, Candy, who seems to care for Eagle, Hillary is much more satisfied when he notices "something odd about her." Odd it is that a white woman would want to be with a black man, particularly in public. She must either be a whore or a mixed-up individual; sound mental health and interracial dating do not go hand in hand. In all likelihood, Hillary might not have glanced twice at Della had she been the girlfriend of another white man. Indeed, his stereotypic vision runs deep, and it causes him always to think the worse about Blacks. For instance, he suspects that Keel, a holder of degrees from Harvard divinity school, must have been kicked out for stealing. That Keel could have left because he was no longer convinced of the relevance of what he learned did not enter Hillary's speculations at all.

Keel offered Hillary a job as a waiter in the nightclub. Confronted by a jazz critic named Crane, Hillary admits to his distaste for working for a black proprietor. His hatred turns on Eagle at one point because a white woman had offered Eagle her body but the musician used her instead of allowing himself to be used. No matter how much the pathos of the nightclub world stirred him, Hillary also had to confess that "something within him nagged that, regardless, he was an outsider, was better than they . . ." (65). This quest to establish superiority retards his ability to respond to the others on an equally human level. Sometimes he feels that *he* is the inferior individual. Regardless of these vacillations, though, Hillary remains constant in his biases. He watches a musician, Kilroy, and thinks:

Kilroy . . . was the way they [black people] all should be. His clothing was loud too. Kilroy seemed to enjoy being a clown. (85)

No satisfaction would come to him until Blacks would act out to the fullest the roles Whites had presumptuously meted out to them. Because the relationship of black and white had historically been one of caretaker (black) and the cared for (white), Hillary almost unconsciously puts himself in a position which would guarantee getting Keel's care and attention. Yet, he simultaneously hoards and despises that sympathy.

The time comes when Hillary has conquered his drinking, has made some money from his waiter's job, and feels ready to rejoin his old profession. He informs Eagle of his appointment with the English department chairman at the University where he formerly taught. Eagle, who expects to be in the University town at the same time as Hillary, suggests that they meet each other. Hillary agrees, but his thoughts reveal his uncertainty about the idea. On the appointed day all goes well with the job interview. The chairman offers him a position, and suddenly, the time spent with Keel, Della, Eagle and the other musicians

. . . was all behind him as though it had never existed; he was back among the softly rolling hills, the bellow from the stadium in the fall, the Gothic edifices, the long, bisecting walks. (118)

All exultations come hurriedly to a halt when, reluctantly going to his rendezvous with Eagle, Hillary bumps into a crowd of students watching a policeman beat Eagle with a club. Apparently, Eagle had been caught loitering and had not explained his presence. Hillary's intervention might have cleared things up. Instead, he kept his distance on the fringe of the crowd, and as the cop swung his stick at Eagle's unresisting body,

Hillary found himself waiting for another blow, just one more to finish out a subtle rhythm; he itched to have the officer strike once more. (119)

Feeling compelled to relate his weakness to Eagle, Hillary goes to his room but cannot suppress a distaste for Eagle. Hearing how his friend had refused to come to his aid, Eagle says to Hillary:

" . . . You won't even help yourself. If you'd taken one step toward me, just one, baby, think what you'd have done for yourself." (136)

Back in New York City and high on heroin, Eagle dons his walking shorts and struts down Fifth Avenue. Hillary follows "trying to keep up and still stay apart." This, after all, was his biggest problem.

Williams has constructed in David Hillary the most striking element of *Night Song,* for it is through the instructor that the novel achieves mythic dimensions. Like heroes of old, Hillary needs to undergo an initiation rite, an initiation into a new knowledge of self which will only come about with a knowledge and understanding of others. Interestingly, he is already a teacher, an occupation which presumes some knowledge, but what he knows must be tempered and molded with an acceptance of his humanity and that of his fellowman. So, besieged by guilt over his wife's death, he sinks into "an area where darkness and dimness gave comfort" (16). The whole Village area of New York becomes somewhat of an underworld with its focal point at Keel's shop which is located in a basement. Keel holds the position of guide for Hillary, like the ominous Charon who ferried the damned across the Styx. Consequently, it will be Keel who will advise and admonish his guest. The environment repeatedly receives descriptions suggestive of a world below the real. For example, there is a constant contrasting of the night and day worlds. Keel takes a cab at night and thinks:

That was sometimes the nice thing about operating at night; at that time New York was filled with Negro cabbies and bus drivers and subway motormen, and they knew what was happening and rolled with it. They had no choice. The day spots went to their white fellow workers. (30)

51

Keel later reflects on how he had met Della

> . . . there in that world of arrogant musicians and worrying night-club owners, a world filled with admirers, detractors, tourists, hipsters, squares, policemen and weirdies, a world in which the days were really nights because you lived mostly in the dark and sang your song of life then. (41)

Della remembered that for the social workers like herself,

> After five o'clock, circulation among the afflicted minorities was frowned upon—even in an office where Negroes, whites, and Puerto Ricans worked together. (51)

Only one of her white female companions would brave entrance into "the shadow world." Hillary, too, felt the night to be "a tranquil stage, where things happened and were absorbed without shock, without feeling" (64). Hence, the night with its murky darkness lent a definition to its black sojourners that is unmatchable in daylight. For the Whites who passed through, they could likewise enjoy the night but never fully appreciate it, for they were not restricted to it alone. The Whites had the best of both worlds and usually took it all for granted. Just as the black subterraneans could come into their element primarily at night, so did black people as a whole find themselves confined to a world that was but a reflection of the white. Surviving in that vicious ghetto became their first order of business. Nor should one imagine that life is easy and always pleasurable there. Too frequently the opposite holds true. Keel knew that should he and Della walk the streets at night they would be stopped at every block and asked ridiculous questions. The night provided more protection for the white cops who would hassle him than for himself. A vicious circle existed. For the black musicians, cabmen, and others who moved at night, an omnipresent desperation overshadowed them. For those who tried to survive in the day, they must accept their near invisibility, that they will often be ignored unless they make themselves menaces. Such was the lesson Eagle learned as he waited for Hillary near the University. On his way there, he is described as "passing like a shadow beneath the darkened elms and maples" (111). Certainly, no one notices him. It is not until he stops and loiters that a cop scrutinizes him to discover whether he belongs there.

If it appears contradictory that Blacks could enjoy the night (which symbolizes an underworld with black inhabitants not equal to that of the day with its white inhabitants) while experiencing a concurrent desperation, it should be recalled that this is a legerdemain long indigenous to oppressed groups.

Here, then, is the world to which Hillary comes for a rebirth, and he comes to the right place. For if one wants to forget one's own pain what better place to go than where misery runs rampant and the sufferers hurt more than one does? Besides, Hillary could console himself that "he was white: thus better: thus sheltered from the coldness at the bottom of the world" (72). He had an alternative Keel or Eagle did not have. Perhaps, this realization corrodes his efforts at understanding and loving his benefactors. When he is asked how he likes working for Blacks, he fumes, wishing he could do something to dispel the prejudices implicit in the question. Why should working for a black man be any different than working for anyone else? Becoming conscious of his anger, Hillary analyzes its cause: "It's because I am a human being—he told himself angrily—that I feel this way" (76). But there's another question to be answered: "Then why—he asked himself—do you feel shame when they ask it?" This question Hillary avoids. Alas, it is the one most needing an answer. "Because I am a human being" would apply to the last question as well. However, here lies his tragic flaw: he cannot accept his humanity and the frailties that attend it if it means his losing his superiority. This attitude blocks his way to a true initiation.

In fact, his whole perspective is tilted. He admits to Keel "that only by being here can I learn to begin to live again" (90). Keel responds that Hillary's experience, then, is like a baptism—of fire, says Hillary; of life, corrects Keel: another revelation about Hillary. He expects (somewhat like young Tarwater in Flannery O'Conner's *The Violent Bear It Away*) a sudden, climactic, earth-shattering conversion which would instantly show him the right path. Unfortunately, such dramatics tend not to occur. Consequently after betraying Eagle and confessing to him, Hillary turns to Keel and Della, gaining solace in their blows. Possibly, an act so violent and tangible is what he thought would salvage him. Keel knows otherwise. To Hillary, he pronounces his doom: " 'Things could've been better . . . But you learned nothing here!' "

The initiation process need not always end successfully, but rarely does one emerge unchanged from it all. Hillary had been warned about the possibility of further retrogression:

> . . . the crazy world of Keel and Della, Eagle and Candy, its utter bleakness, had made him realize that possibly here at the very end—he did not delude himself with his whiteman's mind: it was the end—he could start back. What Crane was telling him now was that there was no end against which he might brace himself and start back. Rod Tolen had told him that, and the restless sadness of Keel and Della underlined it for him. (53)

It did not take long for him to forget this. Once re-admitted into the security of the English department, he discards the world to which he went for rehabilitation. When he does think of meeting Eagle, he does so with an aim to use him. He would show Eagle around the campus, impressing the Department chairman with his "new-found humanitarianism." Indeed, all is a sham, and when Williams describes how Hillary "picked up speed going downhill" from the campus, the *downhill* applies equally to his physical and moral motion. Watching Eagle's demise simply highlights his decadence. In another setting he had instinctively rushed to assist Eagle in a nightclub brawl, but he refuses to render aid publicly and in daylight. Hillary will take no rash steps with job and security at stake. Instead he rationalizes this way: he would like to help Eagle but he is not in the black section at night where there's a total disregard for conventions; he is not "in that isolation in time and space which impelled one to act basically, to take an eye for an eye . . ." (119). So, he watched Eagle being clubbed, feeling "guilty but somehow joyous."

After Eagle's death, Hillary acknowledges the possibility of his [Hillary's] being partially responsible. Ironically, it was a death (of his wife, Angela) which brought Hillary to the "shadow world" and it was a death (of Eagle) which led him from it. In the first case, he had unfairly blamed himself; in the second he was more blameworthy than he might care to admit. No, he had not moved forward; his initiation had not delivered him any ameliorating insights. Rather it had led him deeper into the recesses of his inexorable prejudices, leaving him to wallow there. What hope lies ahead for him? The author concludes the book with these words:

Someday Hillary would understand. Maybe. The bus edged through the toll booths, down the brick road into the gaping mouth of the tunnel. (159)

There is hope, but first Hillary will have to undertake another journey to the underworld. The tunnel will lead to a world different from Eagle's but it will be taxing in its own way. Will he fare any better? Williams' dubious answer is all there is.

The study of David Hillary reveals much of the ambivalence toward Blacks of which the white man, try as he may, can not divest himself. Like a schizophrenic, he assumes the benevolent role only too often finding himself refusing really to give, risk, sacrifice, or love. The shades of night in which Hillary moves are more than just the antithesis of day, or the dichotomy of the black world against the white; it is the very split of the white consciousness, divided against itself. Integration, Williams implies, both mental and racial, is the key to the white—and black—man's salvation.

Keel and Della's ordeal matches Hillary's, though they are more fortunate. They triumph where Hillary fails. Keel had garnered the status his parents craved for him by getting degrees from Harvard. Along with satisfaction over his accomplishments came guilt. He began to perceive that his father (a bishop) was interested in religion chiefly for the status it brought him. Keel had attended Divinity school but had left convicted that "when belief became institutionalized, the seeking ended." Enraged by his disenchantment with religion, with a society which discriminated against Blacks, with the tough night world he had joined where "mercy and kindness were camouflaged in sarcasm, irony, or a bellicose pessimism" (42), and indignant that he was not left alone to love Della because she was white and he black—enraged by all this, Keel becomes sexually impotent. This adds, expectedly, additional tension to the association with Della since his manhood, sexually and racially, is at stake. Caught in a quandary, he fluctuates between love and hate, between a thoughtful wisdom and impetuous presumptions. To illustrate, he can lecture Hillary about his superiority complex, yet Keel must admit that for himself Hillary is an essential tool:

> Hillary stays . . . because he is important to me also . . . I need Della as well as he does to prove that I, too, am a man—a man superior to him. If he takes Della, and he won't, the bastard, then he proves himself in his eyes, as I do in mine, superior to me. (96)

He can fume inside because Whites tend to disbelieve that he and Della could have a normal, healthy relationship. Yet, he cannot readily accept the possibility that Candy, a white socialite, might honestly love Eagle.

Della strengthens Keel through her presence, patience and persistent hope. The author goes out of his way to convince the reader that her love for Keel is wholesome and legitimate. She knows that she plays a part in the impotence of the man she wishes to marry. She knows that although he has been afflicted for a year, she must "deny the selfishness which makes up a major part of love." Like everyone else, however, she is human; which is to say, she is not flawless. She has sex with Hillary, but cannot make the act anything more than an empty exercise. Finally, with the confluence of Hillary's betrayal and Eagle's death, both Keel and Della see the paths they must follow. For Keel it was practicing the perseverance of Sisyphus:

> . . . you were required by the very nature of living to try again, and again, and still again—like climbing a hill only to stumble halfway up and tumble down. You rose and began again. (71)

For Della it meant a ready submission to being disowned by family and friends in order to belong fully to Keel. It meant her inspiring him, and his promising never to stop believing in himself. Their external plight had not changed that much during the course of the novel. What had changed were their attitudes. They accepted their weaknesses, decided to pool their spiritual resources, and hoped for the best. With a cautious optimism Keel can say:

"It always seems to be night when we do anything, like it isn't for real, any of it. It'd be nice, just for the hell of it, to see what it's like to go to a movie on a Saturday afternoon." (156)

He now stands a chance of being able to toss off the shackles of night and to confront courageously the austere realities of the day world. Before approving too strongly of Keel, the reader might well ponder a comment by Hillary who was not as successful at re-orientating himself. He says, " 'A man like Keel doesn't have the choice. He can't be a coward; he's got to make it.' " It's the same old story of the oppressed becoming morally stronger, more defiant while the oppressor grows anemic, sluggish, and feeble.

What about Eagle? Is *Night Song* not his story? Yes it is, but only incidentally. Eagle serves, more or less, as a symbol of victimized talent gone astray. Richie Stokes grew up hard in St. Louis. (Williams' unpublished manuscript, *Bird,* documents the rough life Charlie Parker had in Kansas City.) As a teenager, he got hooked on heroin. More than once was he left for dead. He had also suffered a nervous break- down. As a result of this type of life, he comprehended at a young age what he could expect. For the white managers and club owners the world was theirs for the taking; for musicians like himself the leavings of the former group would have to do. White businessmen exploited Eagle whenever they could. The white female tourists who visited his haunts sometimes offered him their bodies, not because he was an appealing human being, but because he represented "the noble, talented savage." Realizing his position Eagle makes no secret of his hatred for the white abusers. His defiance infected other black musicians. Ultimately, he symbolizes both the victim and the rebel. His philosophy is plain:

"I ask no man to do anything for me except to let me live: let me live my life, without hurting anyone else: let me live and enjoy it." (136)

57

Harboring no illusions about his place in society, Eagle adopts, in defense, a hedonistic and apathetic temperament. Keel testifies to his heroic station among the Blacks:

> "Everybody uses Eagle . . . who is—believe it or not—so much a part of us. We dig the NAACP, even when we laugh at it. But it's impersonal. Some people preserve statues and old drawings on cave walls, but we have to have Eagle. He's fire and brain; he's stubborn and shabby; proud and without pride; kind and evil . . . Eagle is our aggressiveness, our sickness, our self-hate, but also our will to live in spite of everything. He symbolizes the rebel in us. No organization can do that. (93)

At a memorial dance for Eagle, the author further credits his influence:

> Up on the stage the artists came on, all very cool, very sure, very cold on the stand, acting not at all the way Keel remembered colored musicians behaving ten, fifteen years before. Maybe that too was something from Eagle. No teeth, no sambo smiles. That might have been his biggest contribution. (152)

In the end, Eagle is found dead in his apartment. The cause of his death is attributed, by the doctors, to an overdose of heroin. Some mystery surrounds his death, nevertheless. Why did Williams leave the matter up in the air? Maybe he did so to complete the characterizations of Hillary and Eagle. One critic elaborates:

> Williams leaves the question [of Eagle's death] open so that his novel's symbolic level, which is sometimes crudely obtrusive, may go into high gear on the last two pages. On this mythic plane Hillary stands for the "good" white man's complicity in racial prejudice; and Eagle for the hero-victim who bestriding the story's violent midnight, in his own words just "got out too far to come back in."[5]

Night Song captures superbly the existence Blacks have been forced to lead. The series of tragedies that produce an addict like Eagle and kill him as well can easily be documented by references to the daily press which record but a small amount of black affliction. But one must become adept at reading between the lines. When Charlie Parker died on March 12, 1955, the *Daily Mirror* ran an announcement a few days later which seemed like a publicity communique for Baroness Nica Rothschild de Koenigswarter. It was at the Baroness' apartment that Parker had expired. Certainly, the aim here is not to indict one newspaper but the whole American media which designedly overlook the daily horrors of black life. Incidentally, a scanning of *The New York Times'* account of the death may provide another possible explanation, conscious or unconscious, for Williams leaving doubtful the circumstances of Eagle's death. One paragraph of the article reads:

At 7:30 o'clock Saturday evening Dr. Freymann found Mr. Parker in satisfactory condition. Forty-five minutes later he collapsed and when the physician returned, Mr. Parker was pronounced dead.[6]

No one is being accused here; rather, the suggestion is that Parker's sudden death might have, however slightly, affected Williams' fantasy and inspired the fictional hint of mystery in regards to Eagle's death.

This second novel of Williams surpasses the first. Granted that all the characters do not come fully alive (and the reviewers have definitely had their day debating which ones do), the author still gives an excellent performance by elevating to a mythic plane the unsuccessful initiation of a White into the wretched world of black musicians. Williams also discerns that Whites and Blacks are plagued by the past; the first desire to return to the historical white-black relationship; the latter want to move away from it. Compare the following passages.

"How could we be unworthy of your love and yet worthy of your confession? It's not only that you don't know where you are, you don't know where we are. Are you at the top looking down or at the bottom looking up? Has someone been playing with mirrors? Who? Or what? Most important, why?"

The Negro came to the white man for a roof or for five dollars or for a letter to the judge; the white man came to the Negro for love. But he was not often able to give what he came seeking.

59

The price was too high; he had too much to lose. And the Negro knew this too. When one knows this about a man, it is impossible for one to hate him, but unless he becomes a man—becomes equal—it is also impossible for one to love him.

It is no coincidence that both statements are so similar. The first belongs to Keel addressing Hillary in *Night Song*. The second comes from James Baldwin's *The Fire Next Time*. The books were published months apart, and certainly, the authors did not collaborate. The truth is that any number of Blacks could have made similar statements, for none of them escapes the scales, unevenly balanced against them, on which they are placed in their relationships with Whites.

Another powerful element of Williams' book evidences itself in his descriptive passages. With apparent ease he translates, for example, the hieroglyphics of the bleating sax, thumping drums and strumming bass, missing no movement of the players:

At the end of the bar the drummer snapped off a tight, commanding roll and Eagle raised the sax to his mouth and moved back a step from the mike. His heavy hands bammed over the keys and the notes hurtled out . . . Eagle closed his eyes once while he chased an idea through the scales and brought it home. The pianist, head down, raced to keep up, and the drummer, mouth open, beads of sweat beginning to trickle down his face, dropped bomb after bomb, a rim shot here and there, and managed to keep up. The bass, a man not quite half as wide as his instrument, fingered the strings serenely, filling in for all of them with a solid thumping beat. (60)

Along with his vivid portrayal of musicians, Williams builds on the night image. To capture the flux and unpredictable fluidity of the funereal existence, he refrains from naming days or telling dates. How long was Hillary with Keel, Della and Eagle? There is no way to tell. Time becomes amorphous in their world. Only one distinction remains sharply drawn, and that is the difference between day and night. The illimitable applications of the night will surely fascinate the reader. Among the associations previously mentioned, the night stands also for the dark, replusive side of man's nature with which man must either come to grips or hypocritically attempt to ignore. The black race and the night are likewise connected, for not until equal rights materialize for all can the black man become a viable part of the day-society.

In sum, *Night Song* incorporates an anguish which transcends *The Angry Ones*. It contains a wealth of psychological probings never attempted in the first novel. Moreover, the world of *Night Song* is more complex; the novelist faces a tougher task; and Williams' effective handling of it all accents his growth since *The Angry Ones*.

*   *   *

In his fourth novel, *The Man Who Cried I Am*, Williams includes a scene in which one of his characters who had been nominated for a writers' award was subsequently rejected with no explanation. The incident is based on the author's experience with *Night Song*; and because it occupies such an important spot in his private life and writing career his response to the perplexing events is being incorporated in full.

Within months after the publication of *Night Song*, Williams received a letter from the American Academy of Arts and Letters announcing his selection for the Prix de Rome, a $3,500 award, including a year's stay in Rome. Following a brief interview with Richard A. Kimball of the Rome branch of the American Academy, Williams received another letter which said he had been passed over for the award. One columnist compended the current speculations:

> Had his nomination been vetoed because he is a Negro? Or did he have some unspeakable defect, like many people in his well-received novel "Night Song"? . . . Mr. Williams's own surmise was that he had been turned down not because he is a Negro, as such, but because he is a Negro who wears a cap and a beard—and who so violates the foursquare "public image" which, he says, the Rome Academy set great store by during their brief talk.[7]

Ms. Blossom Kirschenbaum who has done remarkable researching of those events of 1962 supports Williams' theory. She describes Richard Kimball as

> a man who seems to have had ideas not just about how a man ought to appear socially, or what sort of work he ought to do, but

61

even some feeling about how an artist ought to look while he was doing his work.[8]

Here, then, is Williams' account which was initially entitled "We Regret to Inform You That" and printed in *Nugget,* December, 1962. (It also appears in *Flashbacks.)* Because of its proximity to the awards, it captures the feeling in a way no backward glance could manage. A valuable and honest piece, it sums up everything pretty well.

Being a writer has very often seemed unreal to me. During the unreal times it was as if I had been afflicted with the *Alice in Wonderland* syndrome—outside myself watching myself move, listening to myself speak, sensing myself think. This springs from my background; there were no writers in my family, only hard-muscled day laborers.

But I accepted what I thought I was when I was recognized by certain constituted authorities as being what I always desired to be. A good writer.

For me this recognition came with a telephone call on January 23rd of this year. The call was to ask if I would be able to accept the American Academy of Arts and Letters Fellowship to Rome for a year. I had made plans which included an associate editorship on a new magazine. In 15 minutes, after having made some calls of my own, one of which assured me of my job with a year's leave of absence, I was able to return the call and accept what is more commonly known as the Prix de Rome, an award which cannot be solicited. My worth as a writer became a reality for me with this recognition, perhaps foolishly so.

On January 31st, a week after the call, I was notified by Douglas Moore, President of the American Academy of Arts and Letters that the AAAL "has chosen you as the recipient of a Fellowship to the American Academy in Rome for the year October, 1962-October, 1963, subject to the approval of the American Academy in Rome."

Mr. Moore's letter outlined the disbursement of the $3,500 award, ($600 transportation, free residence at the Academy, $150 for books and supplies, $500 for European travel, $500 for services performed by the Academy, and the balance of $1,750 to be paid in monthly installments) and ended with, "May I offer you my warm personal congratulations upon the action of the Academy."

When I wrote to Mr. Moore, asking for more information, I included a wow! in my letter. Undignified, sure, but honest; it was the way I felt. In answer to my letter, I received one from AAAL dated February 7th, in which Mr. Moore's assistant said, "I hope that by now you have had an interview with the Director of the Academy in order to make this appointment definite."

I had not been told that I had to have an interview. I called the AAAL and the personnel there set up an interview in the Manhattan offices of the Academy in Rome. I looked with suspicion upon certain phrases in the correspondence—"pending approval of Rome," and "to make this appointment definite," but I was advised by those who should know that these were mere formalities. After all, no one wanted an absolute nut running about, Fellow or not. I was further told that no one who'd been awarded the Prix de Rome had ever had it withdrawn.

I had my appointment with Mr. Richard A. Kimball, Director of the Academy in Rome, on February 15th. I want to go into the following details before getting into the interview because they may have been important:

I do not like hats, because they always strike me as being too goddamn formal, but I have some slight sinus trouble during bad weather. That is when I wear caps. I have a rather Mephisthophelean beard which I wear because I have a grossly receding chin. The image of a guy walking into a Park Ave. office wearing a rakish cap and satyr-like beard should not be dismissed.

I found Kimball a ruddy man with a mustache, I think, and glasses, and good strong teeth which may or may not have been his own. My first impression was that he was dapper because beneath his tweeds he was wearing a gold-colored waistcoat. We shook hands.

Kimball said he'd started reading *Night Song,* my novel which came to the attention of the AAAL and won me the award. I said I hoped he'd enjoy it. He asked if I'a ever done social work, and I admitted that I'd done some. His question made me wonder if he were trying to square what he'd read so far about narcotics-addiction, jazz, interracial love, with a nice, clean-cut colored American boy who had absorbed the material in the book legitimately. I truly think he was trying to see me as this in spite of my cap and beard. With us during the interview was Miss Mary T. Williams, the gray-haired Executive Secretary of the American Academy in Rome.

Kimball asked about my life, my writing. I told him I'd been conceived in Syracuse, born in Mississippi and raised in Syracuse, which is true, but in retrospect perhaps I should not have said so. He did not laugh. My health, mental and physical? Good. The Academy, he told me, was a rather small place. The Fellows lived in rooms, took their meals together, etc. It was very necessary to fit in. I told him I had had a two-week scholarship to the Bread Loaf Writer's Conference in Vermont and had some idea of what it was like. I also indicated that three years in the Navy had taught me the knack of getting along. Most of the Fellows, he went on, were a great deal younger than I, but knowing that Fellows much older than myself had been at Rome, I said nothing. Kimball gave the impression that Fellows were like lesser American ambassadors; the Academy liked for them to get about among the Europeans. This was to my liking: I have a strong distaste for confinement.

When we discussed writing, I let Kimball know that I'd begun work on a novel which dealt with the Roman Empire and ancient Palestine. Not only I thought, could I look up material on Augustus and Tiberius in Rome itself, but the Academy would serve as a jumping-off place for Israel, for this novel will move in the shadow of the Christ story. Toward the end of the interview, which lasted about 15 minutes, Miss Williams and I talked of the best ships to take to Italy—those of the Italian Line or the American Export Line.

The interview ended rather abruptly, I thought. And I had detected what seems in retrospect to have been some uneasiness on Kimball's part during my talk with Miss Williams about the ships.

My next letter was not from American Academy in Rome (an institution chartered in 1905 by Congress), nor from the American Academy of Arts and Letters, but from the National Institute of Arts and Letters. This was the lead paragraph: "You will shortly hear from the American Academy in Rome stating why the recommendation of the American Academy of Arts and Letters that you be elected a Fellow was not approved."

The letter went on to point out that I now, however, would receive a grant of $2,000 from the NIAL, parent body, for my contribution to American literature. After that, a letter of March 2nd from Miss Williams of the Academy in Rome said in part: "We regret to inform you that another candidate also recommended by the American Academy of Arts and Letters was awarded the Fellowship in creative writing."

There was no explanation.

Mr. Roger Straus, President of Farrar, Straus and Cudahy, publishers of *Night Song,* then wrote the NIAL:

"It should be noted that the letter (of March 2) gives no explanation of why Mr. Williams was rejected, but seeks to give the impression that there was no rejection, but rather a choice between two possible candidates. Both your earlier letters, however, make it clear that Miss Williams' letter is an evasion of the facts. We recognize that the NIAL wishes to make clear to Mr. Williams through its recent grant of $2,000 that it does not share the opinion of the Academy in Rome (whatever that is). And though we appreciate this sign of confidence, it by no means alleviates the injury that has been done him . . . We insist that some explanation is owed him, and us as his publishers, as to why this honor which was to be conferred upon him was so suddenly withdrawn."

Straus was on very solid ground. Of three final candidates for the Fellowship, I was unanimously chosen first. The jury included such distinguished writers as John Hersey, Dudley Fitts, Louise Bogan, Phyllis McGinley, S.J. Perelman, Robert Coates and John Cheever. There was not, as I understand the material which has come into my hands, a choice for the Academy in Rome to make; it could only make a rejection and it did.

Douglas Moore, President of NIAL, partially confirmed this when he answered Roger Straus' letter on March 14th: "My notification to Mr. Williams was premature, and I apologize to him although' he was first on our list as originally submitted."

It is my belief that if Farrar, Straus and Cudahy—from receptionist to boss—had not stepped in to register complaint, the deed would have remained underground with similar others that must be perpetrated in this foundation-and-fellowship area every year.

Now, let's hang out the wash.

If a rejection rather than political juggling took place, it could only have been on two counts—racial or political or both.

There is a very real possibility that the rejection was based on political considerations. We all should know by now that there are lists upon lists in the power palaces, of people who are, who might be, and who have been, you-know-what. There are also lists (Dirty Lists, they're called) of persons who have been associated with the people in all these categories, knowingly or not, willingly or not.

Now, of all white institutions I detest politics the most. Politics has made an Augean mess of the few basically good concepts that brought this nation into being. There are too many men who, with too little equipment, have come to this place of power simply because millions of people—black people—have had no voice in the matter. And this is a condition these little men with little equipment fear to see altered.

But to move on, in 1960 I was hired to put on a rally as a fund-raiser by the New York Chapter of the National Committee for a Sane Nuclear Policy. The Rally was a success even though the Dodd Committee was on the prowl for Communists before, during and after it. There were a good many volunteers and I worked with most of them. I talked to people from *Tass* and the *Daily Worker;* I talked with people from the *Times* and *Tribune* as well. In the course of putting together what was then the largest concerted protest against nuclear testing and assembling the largest delegation for peace, I talked to many people. My name went out on letters and press releases, checks and so on. Proudly. I don't know if the phones were tapped, but I wouldn't have been surprised; very little surprises me about America, and a great deal angers me. Yes, I believed then and still do, in a moratorium on nuclear testing; yes, I believe in peace.

I was not among those people subpoenaed by the Dodd Committee after the Rally. But I had certainly been associated with some who had been called before the Committee. Who was what politically, I didn't know, didn't ask, didn't care. When the Rally was over

I went looking for work among the very institutions where one's politics were not supposed to matter. I learned then that I was not supposed to be "a good risk" because of my participation in the Rally.

If the rejection by the American Academy in Rome was based on these political associations, the wrong was no less than if I had been rejected on racial grounds.

So here I am face to face with that other possibility. We first must admit that it is no longer fashionable to be publicly anti-Negro, which may explain the lack of communication between myself and Rome. It is said that even the better, moderate people of the South feel it is bad taste to be anti-Negro out loud, and that it is the rabble who do not care for fashion or taste who are raising all the hell. Perhaps. But I for one am weary of hearing about the good, moderate white people North and South, who stand in the shadows waiting to be interviewed by *The New York Times*. I don't think they exist. If they did or do, surely they have had time enough and room enough to make their stand if indeed they wanted to make one.

Which brings me to Mr. Kimball who, as far as I know, is not a Southerner, but a product of the liberal North. It is my considered opinion that this entire affair pivoted around his acts. I do not mean to give the impression that Negroes have never gone to the American Academy in Rome, they have. Ralph Ellison, the novelist, and Ulysses Kay, the composer, are two who readily spring to mind; and there have been two others. Kimball has been at Rome two years. Negroes have not been there under his tenure.

Earlier I mentioned that I wore a cap going to the crucial interview. This, together with the beard, the authorship of *Night Song* and being a Negro in the bargain, might have broken it. While race I am now positive was the largest contributing factor in the rejection, there were other things, such as a lack of "proper background." (I did not go to an Ivy League School.)

The vast silence—the awful, condoning silence which has surrounded this affair fits a groove well worn. Though the NIAL and the AAAL and many of their members might have suffered some embarrassment, I remain the single person most affected. I spoke

67

of the affair fitting a groove well worn. I mean that the rejection confirms suspicisons not really ever dead, confirms an inherent distrust and makes my "paranoia" real and therefore not paranoia at all. That is the sad thing, for I always work to lose it. It is costly and sometimes crippling to have about. But I would be an ass, wouldn't I, to toss my armor into the moat while the enemy continues his charge?

In my new novel, *Sissie*, I say something about Whites expecting Blacks to absorb blow after blow and go off to Harlem or Bedford Stuyvesant (Brooklyn's black belt) and nurse their wounds or die, but not to complain about them. I believe my experience with the award gives more truth to that statement than I dared think possible. Having thought and thought, having seen the program for the joint ceremonial of the NIAL and the AAAL, which listed my name as one of the recipients for the $2,000 "consolation prize," I changed my mind. Although my financial need was great and I flirted with the idea of coming away from this mess with *something,* my ultimate decision was to turn down the $2,000.

On May 7th, in a letter to Douglas Moore, I said: "I feel now that were I to accept the award it would be tacit agreement that no explanation (for my rejection) was due me. I regret to inform you, therefore, that I must decline the award." Mr. Moore, in answering my letter, merely said that the Grant would be "in effect and available until the end of the year," and expressed his disappointment that I wouldn't cop the bread. Moore noted that he was requesting the President of the Rome Academy, not Director Kimball, to write me. Further, Mr. Moore told me in his letter that my name would be removed from the Ceremonial program if I did not reconsider within a few days. I responded to this last by asking him not only to leave my name on the program of the Ceremonial, but to read aloud my letter declining the award as well. I felt for a time that I was about to be made invisible, non-existent. And I am very much alive.

Meanwhile, back at the ranch, I got a letter from the President of the Rome Academy, Michael Rapuano, who assured me that any racial charge against the Academy was unfounded. Rapuano admitted that I *had* been the first choice, but that the second candidate, poet

Alan Dugan, "would profit more from the year in Rome than would you." This apparently was the long-awaited explanation.

But it explained nothing.

By declining the Grant in Literature I had suddenly become a bad boy; I was making waves and that embarrassed The Establishment. What Allan Morrison of *Ebony* has called "the silken curtain" descended. There was some newspaper coverage about the incident, but in most places the stony silence continued. Reporters Barrett and Adbury of the influential *New York Times* were on the story, but it was never filed. Farrar, Straus & Cudahy were told that the *Times* definitely would not be running the story. And all my life I had wanted to make *The New York Times!*

That was the picture on the day of the Ceremonial. Malcolm Cowley, President of NIAL, told the fashionable gathering that I had declined the Grant because of some "misapprehension" concerning the Prix de Rome. He did not elaborate and I leave it to you to decipher what he meant. My letter declining the award was not read. The affair seemed to have been successfully glossed over. And it would have been had it not been for Alan Dugan.

Now, much to the dismay of the officials of the Ceremonial, he rose to his feet and explained that I had declined the Grant in Literature because I had been rejected as the Rome Fellow. He told his audience that he had been the second choice. Dugan said that in the confusion created by the situation he would "take the money from the AAAL and go to Rome in the hope that the AAAL would behave better in the future."

Dugan said that if the panel of judges had been firm in its choice of myself, the "painful mess" could not have happened. Dugan, winner of the National Book Award and the Pulitzer Prize—both for poetry, brought the issue into the open. He was offered many congratulations for his act. Had it not been for this calm, rather lean gray-haired man, the issue would have remained behind the closed doors of the officials of the Institute and Academy. And if it had not been for Dugan the press might have continued to hang about on its haunches. Even the noble *Times* had to do something. Further, Dugan's statement, which startled more than one honored guest, forced Malcolm Cowley to state publicly that the contractual relationship between the American Academy of Arts & Letters and the Rome Academy would be "reviewed."

Those involved in the behind-the-scenes transactions did such a good job of concealment that Dugan did not come into possession of the facts about the Farce de Rome until 24 hours before the Ceremonial. I sincerely hope that Dugan will not incur any of the hostility of which many of the Literary Powers are capable. I hoped from the start that he would not be involved. But as he told me, he was involved and intended to act. It seems to me a damned shame that of all the people somehow involved, only Dugan was capable of acting when it counted.

However, it's all over; the awards have been presented and the furor has died. I am glad, for the experience left me drained and cautious. But I found many new friends—men cut out from the boys and women cut out from the girls. There was a gain after all. And I learned a valuable lesson; self-recognition, that thin line between arrogance and self-confidence, is infinitely more important than public recognition. This was a difficult and painful lesson to learn. But while I have forgiven those responsible for the experience, I can't forget.[9]

Eventually, Williams did accept the $2,000 grant. Later in the year the American Academy discontinued its prize for literature. As announced in *The New York Times,*

John Hersey, secretary of the American Academy, said the board of directors could not ask their own juries to make nominations for grants or fellowships that are subject to review by any other organizations. (October 9, 1962, p. 44.)

1962 was indeed a strange and trying year for Williams.

Notes to Chapter Three

1. John A. Williams, *Night Song* (New York: Farrar, Straus & Cudahy, 1961). Subsequent references will be to the 1970 Pocket Book edition.
2. Bruce Cook, "Writers in Midstream: John Williams & James Baldwin," *The Critic,* (Feb-March 1963), p. 36.
3. Feather, rev. of *Night Song* by John A. Williams, *Downbeat* (4 January 1962).
4. N.S., "A Gem of a New Novel on Music (Jazz), People (Negro and White)," *People's World* (13 January 1962).
5. C.A.B. (initials only given), "An Angry Look at Life," *Buffalo Evening News* (25 November 1961).
6. "Charlie Parker, "Jazz Master Dies," *The New York Times,* (15 March 1955).
7. Hallowell Bowser, "A Season of Discontent," *Saturday Review* (6 October 1962), p. 23.
8. Blossom Kirschenbaum, "Prix de Rome: The Writing Fellowship Given by the American Academy of Arts and Letters in conjunction with the American Academy in Rome, 1951-1963." Diss. Brown University 1972, p. 76.
9. "We Regret To Inform You That," December 1962 issue of *Nugget* from *Flashbacks* (New York: Doubleday, 1973).

Four

Aunt Jemima is Dead: Sissie

With the fiasco of the Prix de Rome behind him, John A. Williams resumed work, and in early 1963 *Sissie*[1] was published. It is the story of young Sissie Peterson who leaves Mississippi to take a job as maid for a white family in upstate New York. Black and poor, she dreams of contracting a good marriage and acquiring the security of a family and home. The pride of the town, symbolically named Bloodfield, is Big Ralph Joplin whose popularity as a singer far exceeds his earnings. Sissie and Ralph marry. Ralph loses his job, has difficulty finding another, and Sissie seems constantly pregnant. Perhaps fortuitously, two of the children die during infancy. Little Ralph, Iris and Robbie survive. Sissie, disgusted with Big Ralph's inability to provide for them, flirts with an old boyfriend. Finally, Big Ralph leaves, and Sissie is left to raise her three children. Strict and quick to chastise, she instills fear and ambition into the two oldest, Little Ralph and Iris. She is determined that they will make their lives the success that hers has not been. Successful as Iris and Little Ralph become, they do not escape the scars. *Sissie* probes the psychological impairment sustained by the siblings as they try to come to grips with what they have become—what Sissie has made them become.

On first glance, *Sissie* may appear loosely structured because of the author's erratic movement through time. There is a method and pattern, however. Part One deals with Iris; flashbacks in this section are usually seen through her eyes. Part Two concentrates on Ralph Jr. and his perspective on the situation, Part Three on Sissie, and Part Four brings the children to Sissie's deathbed. This does not mean that the reader gets one story told three times in Faulkner-like fashion. Iris has a side unknown to the others; her brother, too, relates events which Iris and Sissie know nothing about; the same applies to Sissie's reflections. Each sheds light on his or her personality and motives. When the final scene closes, the reader is not surprised at the outcome but disheartened because things could not have been otherwise.

The novel begins with Iris returning to America from Europe where she has lived for thirteen years. A famous singer, in the mold of Josephine Baker, she is ostensibly at home in her luxury.[2] Nevertheless, memories of past poverty haunt her. Her brother, Ralph, is a noted playwright and she a celebrity, but she can recall the time when

> every other Tuesday she and Ralph had gone to pick up their ration of government-issued surplus food during the Depression: tinned beef, dried prunes, grapefruit, wheat, oatmeal, apples and everything marked with the telltale stamp. (6)

Iris now wears expensive shoes but

> She remembered also those rare, enthusiastically welcomed parades to the Modern Boot Shop where new shoes, restricted in style, colors and durability by the yellow welfare order in Sissie's bag, were obtained for them. (13)

This deprivation causes the thirty-two-year-old singer to search out frantically the best footwear available; as if to make up for the years she had used newspaper to cover the holes in her shoes.

No sooner is she off the plane than Iris encounters the racism that she had wanted to forget existed in America. She is searched for drugs while her white friend passes undisturbed through Immigration checkpoints.[3] Ralph meets her at the airport, takes her to his home, where they await better weather—a snowstorm threatens air travel—to go to Los Angeles. For it is there that Sissie lies deathly ill.

Examining Iris' relation with her husband, Harry, and a boyfriend, Time, reveals much about her character. Equally as wide-eyed and hopeful as Sissie had been when she married Big Ralph, Iris weds Harry and accompanies him to Germany where he is stationed as an army lieutenant. Soon disgusted with the routine of social gatherings and officers' wives' gossip, she begins to yearn for her first love:

singing. Harry, of course, will not permit his wife to exhibit herself in a nightclub. Iris becomes increasingly incensed as

> her life remained static, deadeningly static. It was clear that Harry didn't give a damn whether she ever sang again. She felt like one of his uniforms, useless except when worn; meaningless until removed from the closet and patted down to conform to the lines of his body. (50)

Sissie has taught her to accept no such conformity. She must be her own woman. By chance, she meets Melvin C. Curry, symbolically nicknamed Time, along with a black combo in a club. After singing a song with them, she receives the most uplifting compliment: an offer to work with the band. Although Iris refuses, her relationship with Harry is at an end. It takes only another inadequate sexual interchange to force matters to a crisis. Sickened because he did not satisfy her, she viciously asserts herself:

> She climbed atop him, pressed her hand tightly against the surface of his shoulders, near his neck. "Be still! Don't move!" (55)

After forcing him to help her reach an orgasm,

> She felt him moving away and when that lovely paralysis ebbed, she looked at him with hard eyes and a defiant smile that showed only around her lips. His eyes were filled with hatred. Her eyes laughed him down. Wordlessly he rose and went off. (56)

Here are the first signs of an aggressive usurpation of the male role which she has acquired from her mother. Leaving Harry, she joins Time's band.

It does not take long for Iris to gain a sense of belonging on the Continent. Turning herself into a success is her sole ambition. Even when her singing attracts large crowds, she pines for the days when she will get individual billing. Like Dreiser's Carrie Meeber turned Carrie Madenda, Iris itches for fame and wealth:

She felt a curious impatience; why was she no further along than she was? How long did it take to become—what? A star. She was a star, but she meant a bigger one; big enough to cause a tight fit to the image she'd already formed for herself. (82)

Time witnesses her relentless craving, guesses her selfishness, but can not help falling in love with her. He waits until she is one of the most sought-after singers in Europe. Then he proposes marriage. Iris rejects him:

"I'm sorry. I've thought about it for a long time."
"You've thought about yourself. You had that when I first saw you."
She said, "Time, I do love you—"
"I know all about *that* kind of love." (89)

Time has figured her right. Iris has been so programmed toward one goal, making herself a success, that she cannot respond to the affections of another human being. Convinced that she is a captive of her own narcissism, Time leaves her. His departure immediately helps her realize how important he is to her. She feels she loves him but is incapable of thinking of him as Time the man. Instead she instinctively perceives him as Time the bandleader who will enhance her stardom. Sometimes she does approach a genuine feeling for him; however, it lasts a short while. For instance, she fantasizes about phoning him. She could say that she was sorry and and beg him to take her back. She quickly halts her dreaming, though, because "she had never, never been like that" (48); never been one to plead, to exhibit such signs of weakness. Indeed, Iris' fear of appearing to be weak turns out to be her major weakness. Because Sissie has been strong and domineering, Iris falls prey to this example.

Another childhood influence may help to explain why Iris does not consent to marry Time. Sissie had spitefully misled Big Ralph into believing that Iris was not his child. To keep up the fiction, she had refrained from showing any public affection for Iris; Sissie did not wish Big Ralph to think that she loved another man's child more than his own children. No doubt Iris grew up believing that affections should not be overtly demonstrated. No wonder she finds it difficult just to apologize to Time. Total commitment, then, is out of the question because she has never received it and has little inkling of what it means. How does Iris feel about Sissie? In a word, bitter; but her bitterness has acquired a calmness over the years. She is no longer actively angry because of the way Sissie acted, but would admit that "she really didn't seem like a mother to me" (30). When Sissie wrote to announce the death of Iris' younger brother, Robbie, in the Korean war, the matriarch said:

Lord, I wanted this family to be a great strong tree, like some of those oaks on your grampa's place. But something is eating that tree from the leaves and the branches right down to the roots. And I just left another branch in the ground. (77)

With more malice than sympathy, Iris thinks, "Poor Mother . . . Poor tree being eaten leaf by leaf, branch by branch, down to the trunk and into the very root" (77). Later, as she attends her brother's play, she deplores Sissie for missing the opening-night performance. Iris' resentment of Sissie runs deep. Perhaps, she could not be expected to return what she was never given.

The problems of Little Ralph, the oldest of Sissie's children, seem to eclipse those of Iris. His childhood was excessively turbulent. He had endured poverty, being abandoned to a children's home, seeing his father attempt to kill his mother, watching a rat nibble his sister's face while strange men trekked in and out of his mother's bedroom. In addition, Sissie's petulance usually vented itself on him; the bruises from beatings were many. Ralph reflects how his joining the Navy probably salvaged his manhood:

. . . he might have turned into a riproaring faggot because Sissie had been that strong. But there had also been the hatred awakened by her beatings. (245)

Rather than instill docility, the punishments strengthened his defiance. Once Sissie flailed him with a broom. Ralph took the broom away from her, stared her down, until she broke into tears. At fourteen, he felt he was then a man. Thereafter he would mistakenly interpret manhood as a constant show of aggression plus an ability to survive independently of others. This false notion that a real man "made his own way" regardless of whom he hurt in the process results from the self-asserting model Ralph had in Sissie. Of course, the author indicts as well the society which leaves little recourse to Sissie other than to be harsh with her children in order to prepare them for the harsh reality of racial discrimination.

Hoping his hometown girlfriend would complement his exhausting efforts to be a playwright, Ralph marries her. Shortly, he and April have a daughter, Raphaella. Then, he notices that April wants to tie him to the routines of family life. Shattered by her lack of interest in his writing Ralph withdraws his affections. To some degree Williams bases Ralph's marital difficulties on the conflict he had with his own wife over writing. Ralph echoes the author's views when he criticizes his wife for wanting him to pursue more secure work than writing, mainly to keep up with the Joneses. Ultimately April and Ralph separate.

Like Obie in *The Angry Ones,* Ralph begins to suspect that there may be some flaw in him which can explain why he has so many difficulties. So, he submits himself to psychoanalysis. During this time, he meets Eve whom he later marries. This second union works out a little better than the first. With Eve's moral support, he produces a successful play, *Shadow on the Sun,* and gains a firmer understanding of the responsibilities of loving and being loved. Again, Williams seems to be saying that the black artist who has enough obstacles because of his race may stand a better chance of success with a mate who understands and appreciates his art rather than one who is primarily concerned with surface signs of security.

The two most telling events in Ralph's life are his confrontation with a white man and his meetings with the psychiatrist. During the war he had been insulted by a fellow sailor called Doughnut, a large and surly White. Each time Ralph would try to get a drink of water, Doughnut would knock him down, yelling "nigger." Ralph admits that " 'he was something evil to me, like a Fate.' " (From then on, Doughnut would be the word he would use to identify the forces in life which he found inescapable and uncontrollable.) Helpless against the sailor's brute strength, Sissie's eldest child saw his only solution; he had to kill Doughnut: " 'I couldn't begin living again until Doughnut was dead.' " But, once he had murdered the bully, he had recurring nightmares about his act. Years afterwards, he had sexual relations with a hometown nymphomaniac, named Jeanette. Obsessed with controlling the love-making to her own fancy, she, too poses a threat to Ralph's manhood. She, too, must be subdued. Ralph asserts his masculinity until Jeanette "was no longer her peculiar kind of a virgin. . . ." Sometimes when he dreamed of Doughnut, the dead man had the face of Jeanette. Translated, all this suggests that throughout life young Ralph, like characters in Richard Wright's stories, felt threatened by occurrences, directly affecting him, which he could not influence one way or another. As long as he was so menaced, he had to do his best to eradicate those events; otherwise his manhood would be questionable. Since Sissie persistently fought the Fates, his surrender would underscore his inability to measure up to her, a woman. Ralph considers his plight:

He wished he were able to get to those ugly gnomes who inhabited the secret control rooms of the world and horse-whip sense into them, the way Sissie had done him. (166)
He was puzzled as well as angry, for he had once felt that he controlled his own life; he had had to. But by pressing open finger after finger of that tightly closed fist, year after year, the Fates had removed his grip upon himself; they had done it snugly, tauntingly. (167)

Where Ralph's reasoning goes astray is that he thinks too frequently of his mother as fighter to realize that her very fighting spirit has fallen victim to the Fates. That is, she struggled to raise successful children. Were not their successes a source for further misery? She wanted them to be happy. Weren't they plagued by feelings of guilt and inadequacy? Maybe his true consolation could not occur until the ultimate irony occurs, when Sussie in spite of all her harsh combativeness succumbs to the ultimate fate—death.

The early triumph of Iris as a singer in Europe does not help Ralph much. She was famous and he was a playwright still in search of an audience. So, there were two women he had to catch up with: his mother and his sister. With his masculinity under such assault from the women in his family as well as from the white society that would not let him be the man or live the life he wanted, it is no surprise that he turns in desperation to psychoanalysis.

Ralph reluctantly relates the shambles of his life. With all the details accounted for, one basic impasse existed:

" . . . I want to live. I want everything that living means. I want to be useful. I want to look at people and not wonder when or with what foot they'll try to kick me in the tail . . . I want to be able to love . . . But there is a force, doc, which activates wherever I go, whenever I do anything or say anything. It says, no." (111)

To compound the feelings of inferiority, he begins to wonder whether his father might also have been a better man than he was credited. Big Ralph had helped when many men would have turned their backs. It was he who had removed young Ralph from the city home. He had forgiven Sissie for her infidelity and accepted her "bastard" child. He had put his dignity on the line to help with family expenses. Ralph, Jr., asks himself:

"Could it be that I'll only see my father when I am superior to him, when I have more money than he, when my position is unshakable?"

Williams implies that white America is mostly to blame for Ralph's quest for superiority. On the one hand the racism which preaches that Blacks are inferior to Whites lay at the bottom of his desire to be superior. On the other hand the circumstances which created the family life in which he feels threatened and inferior relates back to the existence of a racist society which would not permit equal social and economic rights to all. Had those rights existed he would not have had to grow up in a fatherless, poverty-stricken home.

Perceiving his patient's myriad difficulties, the doctor finally makes his diagnosis. One, Ralph is afraid to love. Says the doctor, " '. . . I think, while you know love is a good thing, you basically feel it's a weakness.' " Two, the acceptance of his play has given a boost to his self-esteem. Three, all the ills he imputes to racial conditions derive, likely, from his own personality. The doctor barely concedes that

> The rationale that his problems stem directly from racial origins may have some validity; patient claimed no adjustment to an inferior status could be made when therapist suggested an acceptance of the reality of the situation . . .(158)

Ralph frustratedly reacts to this last view of the analyst.

> "We've been making it in circles. You say it's *me;* I say it's *it.* You talk of *your* reality, the one you know as a white therapist. I'm talking about *mine;* mine as a black man and we're not talking about the same reality." (152)

Ralph insists that his personality was molded by his race. He expands on the deterministic role of his skin color.

> "At every bend in the road there's been *it,* for me, for my family, all the way down the line, . . . Do you think my parents would have been at one another's throats if there'd been room for my father to behave even nominally like a man; do you think he enjoyed living a life without balls, letting his wife bring home the bacon? And further, would my mother have been my mother if they had allowed my grandfather to live his life a man instead of a black man down there in Mississippi. The last recession—why are ninety percent of the men out of work nonwhite? You ask me to adjust to these conditions? The things which constitute your reality are nothing more than a psychic concentration camp for me . . ." (152-153)

Puzzled and still unconvinced, the therapist sheepishly asks of a colleague: "Is there really anything to Tappan's pilot study on the effect of discrimination upon Negroes?"

Although the author attaches tones of earnestness to the debate between Ralph and the psychiatrist on the question of race versus personality, the reader may likely get the impression that Williams was parodying the whole argument. The matter is not so simple, though, and the ease with which the analyst clings to his preconceptions underlines the sad humor of many intelligent Whites who find comfort in believing that racial problems are in the mind.[4] Nor is personality completely absolvable. Some of Ralph's difficulties do come from his particular approach to life since personality and race are indisputably related. Hence, in miming the ancient exchange on race, Williams laments that such abundant social inequities should occur at all, much less the need to bicker over causes.

Sissie, who forced herself into the forefront of Ralph's and Iris' lives, recollects how she had denied herself for her children. Her disillusionment had been enormous. The white "Christian" family she worked for acted as if she were a mindless, feelingless slave. Then, the North abounded in prejudices as much as did the South. Her marriage to Big Ralph lost its glitter because of their meager income.

At one point after her husband lost his job, she finds herself grateful that one of the children dies—it would be one less mouth to feed. Finally, she accuses Big Ralph:

" . . . I'm not the man in the house; *you're* the man, but you don't act like it. *Some*body's [sic] got to be the man here and make some money to bring in here, and it sure ain't you!'' (202)

She wonders:

At what point had she become the man and he less than the man he seemed to be? . . . She needed someone who had been untouched by this decay, this hopelessness, this chaos—someone who would make her feel like a woman instead of a drayhorse. (202, 203)

Big Ralph tries to explain to Sissie that he could not find employment until be became " ' . . . pretty good at suckholin' around.' '' But no matter what his poverty, a man had to keep self-respect, '' 'That's all a poor man has, his damned pride, which he can't give his family to eat' '' (182). His protestation only partially satisfies Sissie. She has been too infected with the idea that the role of supporter, allocated to man, was essential if a man were to hold on to his manly status. (A similar view causes so much trouble for Little Ralph.) Moreover, the pressures of racial discrimination do not placate her anxieties. Williams presents here a classic situation of the emasculation of the black man. Blacks are often so constricted economically that the man finds himself feeling inadequate and less of a man because he cannot provide for his family. And Sissie does not help when she refuses to understand her husband's need for dignity: a dignity he receives neither on the menial jobs available to him nor in the home where she constantly belittles him.[5] Not surprisingly, she one day finds Big Ralph gone.

On her own, she sets out to teach her youngsters that life is rough, that they would have to be better than the next fellow to survive, and that a driving ambition would take them a long way. As the reader has come to expect, she does not perform her duties uncomplainingly. She dislikes having to deny herself comforts for the children's sakes. She grumbles about her condition and accuses Big Ralph:

> Was this the meaning of her life, to have kids who didn't obey her, to work her fingers to the bone just to keep the crumbs in their mouths and rags on their backs? Big Ralph was free now, no good, shiftless. Didn't want the responsibility of a family. *She* had come back. (233)

Feeling herself a martyr, Sissie vacillates between a strictness, when she would beat Little Ralph without any "sense of time and of reality" and a carelessness, when she would "lose herself in a succession of lovers." The author makes it clear that her ambivalance toward her maternal duties was normal but that she carried it to the extreme.

When Iris and Ralph are still youngsters, Sissie meets Oliver Duncan. They marry, move to Los Angeles, and there life improves. They finally acquire such security symbols as car and home. She feels she has reared her children well and deserves her new life. However, she is getting old and Williams questions whether the life she has lived and the torture through which she has put her children through were worth it. Surely, she has had little choice in the matter since she was a mere product of her society. Sissie deludes herself into thinking that any indiscretions on her part would be forgiven by Iris and Ralph. She was in for a surprise.

The concluding scenes of Sissie may well prove, as one critic puts it,

> shattering to readers accustomed to charitable milk and honey death bed departures that close with soft tears and a gentle sigh . . .[6]

Ralph and Iris fly to Los Angeles to spend with Sissie the last minutes of her life. En route, both children assess their lives and their mother's influence. Iris thinks back to Sissie's shouting and prophesying that they would not amount to anything. This was her way of urging them to show her differently.

> Well, they had shown her. Only she hadn't been there to see. If only she'd been present at Berns that night . . . [sic] Well. She hadn't even come to New York for Ralph's opening. Sissie hadn't given them the pleasure of being present; it was as if none of it had counted for anything. (257)

Iris blames her mother for a lack of interest in the success of Ralph and herself as well as for the loss of Time. Because she has been taught to be so success-oriented, Iris let the man she loved slip through her fingers. She may not have been condemned to a loveless life had Sissie herself shown more love and compassion.

Ralph doubts the value of his and Iris' prosperity. They can not elude a guilt for having achieved what the majority of Blacks could not. Ralph ponders their position:

> Can you think about being back home with all the broads you grew up with and not feel goddamned guilty about having made it? It makes me feel bad; it makes me feel as though they hate the hell out of me. You can feel it: a word here, a look there, like you were—not a criminal—oh, I don't know. Like a white folks' nigger. To a Negro, you know, that's worse than being a criminal. (259)

He realizes, though, that Sissie may not deserve all the blame. For whatever one does or becomes, "it always cost." Had circumstances been different, he would have still had to pay a price for that difference. Dying from a heart attack, Sissie regains consciousness as Iris and Ralph approach her bed. Her last desire was to ask Iris' forgiveness for not admitting that she was Big Ralph's child and to see her son's wife, Eve. So, she appeals to Iris who refuses to respond. The one thing Sissie has given her is "the right to refuse." Ironically, she chooses to exercise this right in her last encounter with her mother. Furthermore, as she observes the dying matriarch, she thinks:

> But no, this was not her mother—this was only an old colored woman who called herself her mother. No mother would have behaved the way Sissie had. (271)

Asked whether he was ashamed to bring his wife, Ralph answers Sissie negatively; but his leaving his wife behind is as much an act of defiance as is Iris' refusal to forgive.

> No, shame had not been involved; he had wanted his wife and his mother to be kept forever separate. Sissie altered in some way everything she touched . . . Through Eve he had found his way to his own life. (272)

Painfully Sissie says,

> " . . . Don't you know what those years were like for me? When you had shoes to wear, I didn't. When you had school paper, I didn't have lunch. I couldn't have a single dream so you could have a little teeny one . . ." (274-275)

With this affirmation of her good intentions, Sissie dies. The siblings go calmly from the room. Ralph's thoughts sum up both their views:

> Ah, Sissie, . . . It cost too much—pain, guilt, hate, rage and much too little love. It was almost too much to demand for the dubious privilege of living. (276)

Iris and Ralph had, indeed, come full circle. They had been raised to be strong, aggressive, tough; and they had felt hamstrung by those qualities. Now they had brought those same qualities, which had armed them for the world, back home to be used against Sissie. Possibly, through her death, they could begin to live. In 1969, *Sissie* was re-issued in an Anchor Books paper edition. An introduction was added by the author.[7] Williams clearly emphasizes what he had hoped *Sissie* would achieve: a picture of the black family and its problems without the customary slants of white social scientists. Several quotes from the introduction would convey the gist of his ideas better than attempts at paraphrasing. Williams concedes a change in the black family since the abolition of slavery:

It is true that black families no longer are being physically torn apart, but the economic grip on black life might just as well be physical; the result, separation, is the same. No black father who believes himself to be a man can remain in or as head of a family group without supporting it. To remain without functioning is to suffer the loss of manhood or, if you will, economic castration. (viii)

What of the stereotypic, jovial and loving black mother who was supposed to be almost saintly, in running a husbandless home?

The white man and his social system, his life style, created the image of the black matriarch, the woman who runs the house in the absence, real or psychological, of the man. Sissie could not be such a stern, sexless, humorless creature. She is vengeful, cunning, and often a fool. She is human and the white image of the matriarch was not. (ix)

About black children:

As for Sissie's children, as all black children, they learn well their lesson of the inherent dangers in white America. But in the learning they are charged to rebel against their conditions and to challenge even their parents. Parents who are members of a minority group insist, often in subtle ways, that their children do what they could not do because of racial restrictions, achieve what they could not achieve in spite of those restrictions. Black parents are much like parents anywhere. They love their children as much as any other; they worry about them. But because they are black the parental burden is greater. With what sometimes appears to be unbearable cruelty, they train their children to survive and even function in the hostile society into which they're born. In the loving then, there is hurt and in the hurt loving. (ix-x)

Other themes interest the author. First,

The question of guilt because of survival and perhaps even success remains one of the uncharted areas of black life. . . . We have asked combat soldiers who've survived the wars, we have asked inmates who outlived the concentration camps, about their guilt about surviving while corpses lay knee-deep around them. But we've not bothered to ask Negroes who are surviving the race war about *their* guilt. (x)

Second,

I also wanted to examine religion to some degree, for it has played a most treacherous role in the lives of black Americans, providing the great escape from reality . . . Ralph and Iris have no choice but to reject religion; it more than anything else made them see its hypocritical posture in both society and their mother. (x)

Sissie illustrates the hostility of black youth towards religion. Once, Sissie tried persuading her son to join the church. Ralph "threw the Bible at her." In a letter to Iris, Sissie prefaces a remark with "God willing"; the phrase summoned a sneer from Iris: "God's will. She wanted to curse, . . ."

All in all, the author has written a novel that lays out the most rudimentary problems of black existence in America. *Sissie* possesses the precision and compactness of a short story. For feeling, for emotional and technical control, no other novel of John A. Williams has so excelled.

Whether *Sissie* will demythologize the black matriarch is a question that cannot be fully determined here. What is a little more definite is that the author has contributed in no mean way a piece of fiction which touches at the heart of humanity, which hints that as the family goes so does the world.

*   *   *

The reviews of *Sissie* in 1963 were mainly complimentary. As usual, some writers bickered over how well the characters in the novel had been drawn. Says one reviewer,

> Williams is capable of more challenging novels of character than this in that Sissie and her children are still more types than they are complex unpredictable individuals.[8]

Says another,

> Mr. Williams has lifted his characters above the stereotypes of too many Negro novels. He has made them people . . .[9]

If these opposing comments invite humor, an unsigned review in the "Courier Book Shelf" of the *Pittsburgh Courier* (February 23, 1963) can only induce wonder. The writer bombards Williams with one negative comment after another until an outright hostility is detectable. The last paragraph capsulizes the mood of the lengthy tirade:

> Too often when reading the times' intellectual output, one feels that too many of these writers have a formula compound of Greenwich Village experimentalism, proletarian themes, the horrors of racial discrimination, the wails of self-pity, and excursions into amorality and sordidness which are more revolting than some others, but he [Williams] is so capable that it is a pity he is unwilling to leave more to the imagination.

The article, a sample of unexplained antagonism a particular writer sometimes receives, was brought to Williams' attention. On March

10, 1963, Williams wrote to George S. Schuyler, editor of the Book Review Department for the *Courier*. The following is an excerpt from the letter:

> Lest you misunderstand, had the review been favorable, I would have been no less interested in knowing who had written it. This practice of publishing unsigned reviews—a rare custom indeed—is inimicable to the standards of journalism as I know and have used them myself. As you are perhaps aware, a reviewer taking advantage of this custom can launch his attacks anonymously. This contrary to the credo which serves as a basis for the survival not only of this nation but of every individual in it, that the accused shall always be faced with his accuser.

It was partly because of such critiques which seemed to proceed from personal biases that Williams abandoned altogether the habit of reading reviews of his books. Besides, he had a conviction that whether favorable or not most reviews contributed nothing much to his growth as a writer. Other incidents would reinforce this attitude. The author tells of a time in 1972 when critics flocked to New York for the National Book Awards week:

> I was on a panel with Ralph Nader and a historian. And all of those assholes, those fucking critics—I think they asked the historian two questions, they asked me a couple questions, but they were asking Nader things like a screw fell out of the dashboard of my car what shall I do, or what shall I do if the thread is wearing thin on the side of one tire of my car. I could not believe it, and yet I knew exactly that this is the way those assholes were. It was incredible.[10]

Before *Sissie* went to press it had two chapters which were subsequently excised. The first, labelled Chapter Six, describes Iris attending a party in New York before Ralph's play was produced, before he had married Eve. As a matter of fact, Eve is still with her first husband Henri Catroux, though she is having an affair with Ralph; and Iris' boyfriend Time is supposed to be in New York as well. The second deleted chapter details the history of Big Ralph and his family from his point of view. Such a slant is never so fully presented in *Sissie* as it was published. Big Ralph, now old, an unreformed beer-drinker, reminisces about Sissie. He knows she is dying, and recalls that she was the only woman he ever loved. The chapter closes with this account:

> . . . Old now, bent. Hair all white. He looked good though, when he was out in his cashmere chesterfield, derby and cane. You'd know right away that he'd once been an old time sport. An all right guy. He'd wanted to go to the cemetery as a mourner when Sissie came to bury Robbie. Big Ralph glanced at his watch as he entered the garage. Four-fifteen. It would be one-fifteen, still night, where Sissie was.[11]

Consideration of these chapters helps the reader to see the direction in which the novel might have gone. For instance, had the first section been kept, an entirely new set of questions would have to be explained; such as, why was Iris back in New York? Would she have eventually contacted Time? Did she try to see Sissie? And if she did see her mother, might not that meeting have mitigated Iris' coldness when she would later approach her mother's deathbed? Rather than attempt to tie the various loose ends this account created, Williams wisely omitted it; instead, he leaves Iris in Europe and settles for a passing reference to the times Little Ralph and Eve shared before their marriage.

The section on Big Ralph informs; even though the story of his family, of his getting a job as musician, and his thoughts about Sissie are somewhat of a drudgery because of its length. If it had been incorporated in the final version of *Sissie,* it might have detracted from the mystery which surrounds him. It might have made Sissie appear more harsh, and lastly, it might have deflected the reader's sympathies from Sissie to himself. Had Big Ralph upstaged Sissie the novel would not be the same. So, the chapter was put aside. Because of these omissions the story maintains a smoothness which would otherwise have been lost.

Although *Sissie,* according to its author, may have received its technical influence from Malcolm Lowry's *Under the Volcano,* it bears resemblance to some books by Richard Wright. As in *Native Son,* there as well as to Wright's own mother in *Black Boy*. There is a preponderance of snow in both novels which emphasizes the naturalistic elements in the works; also it throws in relief the characters' efforts at survival in frigid, often sterile environments. Furthermore, Ralph's rebellion against his mother and society reflects that of Bigger's. Both characters are victims of circumstances; this is confirmed by the events surrounding the murder each commits. The agony Ralph felt from being placed in a children's home echoes Wright's experience. Nonetheless, it is entirely possible that all these similarities may be coincidental. is a rat scene; though Williams does not include so lively a chase. Then, Sissie herself seems related in ways to Bigger Thomas' mother as well as to Wright's own mother in *Black Boy*. There is a preponderance of snow in both novels which emphasizes the naturalistic elements in the works; also it throws in relief the characters' efforts at survival in frigid, often sterile environments. Furthermore, Ralph's rebellion against his mother and society reflects that of Bigger's. Both characters are victims of circumstances; this is confirmed by the events surrounding the murder each commits. The agony Ralph felt from being placed in a children's home echoes Wright's experience. Nonetheless, it is entirely possible that all these similarities may be coincidental.

An incidental note—a brief reference is made to Sergeant Moody as being one of two survivors of a black platoon. Gideon Moody had been the protagonist of an unfinished novel of 1960, called *Moody's Squad*. In that work, Williams illustrates the problems of black troops: They had to combat the enemy as well as their white comrades. One member of Moody's squad is a pianist named Time. Time is the same as the one in *Sissie;* and Moody becomes a model for the main character of a future novel, *Captain Blackman*. Moody and Time exemplify Williams' habit of having his favorite characters reappear throughout his works.

*   *   *

Another early writing serves as a kind of analogue to *Sissie*. A short story, "Son in the Afternoon," appears in *The Angry Black*[12] which Williams edited in 1962. The anthology consists of pieces he felt would best thrust the realities of black misery before the eyes of the reading public. "It is most imperative," the author maintained, "that the Negro be seen and seen as he is; the morality of the situation will then resolve itself, and truth, which is what we all presumably are after, will then be served." Ralph Ellison, John Howard Griffin and James Baldwin were some of the writers included.

"Son in the Afternoon" is a semi-fictional account of a young black man's disgust with the affection he sees his mother, a maid, lavishing on a white child. Wendell, the main character, admits his jealousy. His brothers and sisters never knew the loving treatment he saw being extended to the little boy who was already gathering that Blacks were meant to be his slaves. When the child's mother returns home drunk, Wendell can hardly resist an amorous encounter. Then, he impulsively determines to let the child see him, a black man, in the embrace of the mother. The youngster should be scarred for life. After executing his revenge, he leaves mother and child with an enormous conflict to resolve.

Williams had lingered months in Los Angeles and undergone experiences more than ample to inspire "Son in the Afternoon." In *This Is My Country, Too,* he was to recall his "short and sorry stay in Los Angeles, a city I despise with all my being." And, he remembers that his mother had spent

> better than half her life in other people's kitchens and bedrooms and bathrooms. Like the mythical Aunt Bessie, she knows more about white people than they can ever know about her. (77)

"Son in the Afternoon" is characteristic of the early writings. It protests with no subtlety the physical and psychical disruption the black family sustains because of economic and social inequality. Like *The Angry Ones* the story places more emphasis on its theme of protest than on its plot. However, it does illustrate the author's intense interest in the rigors of the black family. And in this regard it foreshadows *Sissie.* Although the novel like the short story draws on actual experiences, the former provides a much more thorough and artistic treatment. From reading "Son in the Afternoon," however, the reader may readily see the germ of *Sissie,* perhaps Williams' best fictional effort.

Interestingly, Williams had written "Son in the Afternoon" during the fifties. While trying to get his first novel published, he had sent the story to various magazines. *Playboy* and *The Atlantic Monthly* were just two publications which rejected it. At times the experience became extra painful, for the replies often indicated the same racial attitudes that he assailed in his story. Phoebe Adams of *Atlantic* serves as an example. She wrote on January 30, 1958:

> The Son story is no go unless run with a picture of the author who, believe me, had damn well better be black as the ace of spades. Since we can't manage that setup, there's no hope here . . .[13]

Ironically, few short stories have emerged in recent anthologies on Black Literature as frequently as "Son in the Afternoon."

* * *

Sissie signaled a turning point for novelist Williams. While meeting with his psychiatrist, young Ralph had elaborated on

> "Racial discrimination . . . Two things happened when you're able to see and say I'm what I am because of racial discrimination. First, when you reach this conclusion, which seems to me inevitable, you're out of dreams, because the dreams you dream aren't applicable to you. Then you begin killing yourself in a hundred little ways. Or, having reached the end of *that* road, you start back, not really knowing what the hell you're going to do, but at least and at last unhampered by delusion. But there's life in understanding finally where you're at." (153-154)

It was this understanding of discrimination that caused Williams to forgive "those responsible" for his being denied the Prix de Rome award but to caution, "I can't forget." It was with this understanding that he accepted in summer of 1963 an offer to travel around the country for *Holiday* magazine. The result of those travels was recorded two years later in *This Is My Country Too.* Trips to Africa, Europe, the Middle East; jobs with television, radio, and *Newsweek*—they all confirmed his understanding of how rampant discrimination was. The writer who would begin his next novel, *The Man Who Cried I Am,* would

93

not have the same patience with the status quo, would no longer be willing to forgive as was the optimistic writer of *The Angry Ones* and *Night Song*. Perhaps, the Prix de Rome affair was not totally responsible for this personal change; but it was one of the sparks that kindled the flame.

As could be expected, Williams' personal change manifested itself in his fiction. In place of the philosophical Keel or the reflective Steve Hill, Williams begins to create individuals, heralded by Ralph Joplin, Jr., who would not let intelligence retard action—even when violent action was needed. From *Sissie* onward, a new militancy would appear in Williams' characters.

The author's metamorphosis coincides with an alteration in the national mood. Blacks were no longer sitting calmly, supposedly consolidating their gains after the 1964 Civil Rights Act. Shouts of ''Black Power'' could be heard, ghettoes erupted, campuses rebelled. A black militancy was upon the land. So, one could guess that had Williams' particular experiences not carried him to a more defiant stance, then the times might have. He had always insisted on how vital it was to be able to dream. This insistence would not change. However, the author, and his characters speaking sometimes for him, would reassess racial discrimination time and again. True, ''there's life in understanding finally where you're at''; but the matter of where you are going still remains to be determined. Williams would attempt to deal with this dubious future in his next three novels.

Notes To Chapter Four

1. John A. Williams, *Sissie* (New York: Farrar, Straus & Cudahy, 1963). Subsequent references will be to this edition unless otherwise noted.
2. Iris' success in Europe appears to underscore America's racism, since as a black woman she stands a better chance of becoming famous and wealthy on the Continent than she does in the U.S.
3. This scene with Iris being searched by Immigration officials while her white friend passes unchecked resembles scenes from early black novels in which black and white

94

friends may board a train together in the North; but when the train reaches the Mason-Dixon line, the Black is sent to the rear and dirty cars, called the Jim Crow section, while his white friend is permitted to remain in the front and more decent part of the train.

4. In *The Man Who Cried I Am,* Williams has another encounter between black Moses Boatwright and a white psychiatrist. Unlike Ralph's analyst who suspects that Ralph may be having mental problems, Boatwright's analyst believes that Boatwright is fully sane. With Boatwright's sanity confirmed, he will be executed for killing a white man. The suggestion seems to be that the racism about which Blacks complain may be diagnosed as being mental or real depending on whatever conclusion is immediately expedient to the white world.

5. See John A. Williams' "Sex in Black and White," *Cavalier* (September, 1963), p. 15, in which the author quotes from Kardiner and Ovesey's *Mark of Oppression.* " '. . . a Negro female loses respect for her spouse whose economic condition prevents him from acting according to the white ideals or prototypes. The unhappy economic plight of the Negro male does not only contribute to the economic dominance of the Negro female, but also makes her psychologically dominant . . . The [Negro] female now has some of the social value attributes of the male and those of the female. The . . . Negro female cannot be "feminine" nor the male "masculine." Their roles are reversed . . . The male fears and hates the female; the female mistrusts and has contempt for the male because he cannot validate his nominal masculinity in practice.' "

6. Lester Goran, "Human Within Their Personality," *Chicago Tribune,* 31 March 1963.

7. Subsequent quotes from the Introduction to the 1969 Anchor Books edition of *Sissie* will be so indicated by its Roman numeral pagination.

8. Nat Hentoff, "Second-Class Citizenship: No Room 'to Behave Even Nominally Like a Man,' " *New York Herald Tribune,* 14 April 1963.

9. Walter Spearman, "John Williams' Characters Create 'Human Heart In Conflict With Self,' " *The Rocky Mount Telegram,* 21 April 1963.

10. From September 28, 1973 interview.

11. To be found in the John A. Williams Collection in the George Arents Research Library for Special Collections at Syracuse University.

12. Williams, ed., *The Angry Black* (New York: Lancer Books, 1962).

13. To be found in the John A. Williams Collection in the George Arents Research Library for Special Collections at Syracuse University.

Five

A Black Act: The Man Who Cried I Am

Many who know the first three novels of John A. Williams will find *The Man Who Cried I Am* (1967)[1] an overwhelming book because of its myriad themes and sub-plots. What Williams did was to gather all the ideas he had explored in his earlier fiction within the covers of his fourth novel. No wonder, then, the book stuns the reader: too much seems to be coming at him at one time. Nevertheless, *The Man Who Cried I Am* is no hodge-podge of themes; rather it relays, for the most part, its messages through media composed of the historical, the surreal and the naturalistic. All this makes for heightened tones of frustration, despair and anger. However, like the previous novels of the author, *The Man Who Cried I Am* excels not because of its confronting racism and discrimination against Blacks but because of *how* this confrontation is handled.

The plot of the novel centers on Max Reddick, a successful black writer, who while dying of cancer travels to Holland to bury an old friend and make peace with his white ex-wife. There he learns of a desperate plan to eradicate Blacks in the United States. Knowing that the discovery has jeopardized his life, he uses his last hours to forward the details of the plan to a confidant in America.

While the plot unfolds, Max thinks back on his life, and his reflection leads to one of Williams' favorite themes: the dilemma of the black writer. In *The Angry Ones,* Obie Robertson and Steve Hill had difficulties surviving as writers because of their color; and Ralph Joplin, Jr. in *Sissie* had to wait until his thirties to receive acknowledgement from the publishers. Yet, none of Williams' characters acts out so forcefully the spiritual travail of the black writer as Max and his close friend, Harry Ames. Harry is the number one black writer according to his critics and readers, most of whom are white. Max admires him, and when they initially meet at a party, their conversation inevitably turns to their craft. Harry submits the following view:

> "I'm the way I am, the kind of writer I am, and you may be too, because I'm a black man; therefore, we're in rebellion; we've got to be. We have no other function as valid as that one . . . I've been in rebellion, and a writer, I guess, ever since I discovered that even colored folks wanted to keep me away from books so I could never learn just how bad it all was. Maybe, too, to keep me from laughing at them. For taking it. My folks had a deathly fear of books." (49)

About the black writer's job, he says,

> " . . . Your job is to tell those people to stop lying, not only to us, but to themselves. You've written and in the process, somewhere in that African body of yours, something said, 'I am—a writer, a man, something, but here for today. Here for right now.' " (50-51)

Such pronouncements do not fall flat; instead they convince. And when Max retorts that thinking the way Harry does could cause one to feel really important, the reader can hardly escape agreeing. According to Harry's perspective, the writer who is black has a social and historical significance outweighing the tellers of tales whose main goal is to delight and entertain. As early as 1963, Williams had been voicing in articles the ideas he attributes to Harry. For instance, the author wrote:

> Novelists would do well to remember that when the works of the scholar-historians create doubt in the researcher's mind, the researcher then turns to literature as a primary source for confirmation or correction. If the truth of a time, a people, a state is not available anywhere else, let it be in the novel.[2]

So, the rebellion of the black novelist must be a rebellion against a history which helped perpetrate horrible injustices against the race.

Meanwhile, his banner must be that of truth as he wages his battle. Once again, then, the reader of Williams' novels encounters the concept of the black writer and history and the necessity that the former be corrective ministers to the latter. This viewpoint is seconded by Max who wonders, "what they wouldn't do, the white folks, to keep you from having a history, the better, after all, to protect theirs" (223). In an argument with a White House aide, Max angrily asks:

" . . . What histories do you read, Gus? Tell me about the history of the American armed forces, and I can show you where Negroes made up the bulk of those economies by being poor or left out of them altogether; tell me about the history of religion in America, and I can show you where, as long as there have been Negroes in this hemisphere, religion has been an absolute lie; tell me about the history of American politics, and I can show you where American politics would be vastly different today if Negroes had had a real voice in them . . ." (306)

Williams' views, which are reflected in Max and Harry's discussions, tell a lot about his writing, about what he tries to accomplish and why he never abandons the contemporary problems of Blacks in his writings. As previously mentioned, the comments by Max and Harry have a convincing urgency that helps the reader to understand why the author is so impatient and relentless in his subject matter.

In Part One, Harry Ames duplicates some of Richard Wright's experiences. Marion Dawes, a young, promising black writer, who seems to be modeled on James Baldwin, says to Harry, " . . . You're the father of all contemporary Negro writers. We can't go beyond you until you're de*stroyed*" (217). Richard Wright had felt that Baldwin was out to destroy him. Williams explains the conflict in *The Most Native of Sons:*

They [Baldwin and Wright] were a generation apart, but they remained victims. They were artists, writers, yet they knew that only one of them at a time, were it James Baldwin, Langston Hughes, Chester Himes, Ralph Ellison, or Richard Wright, could be, would be allowed to be, the black writer of the moment. America was not geared

99

nor did it wish to be geared for the spectacle of more than one black writer at a time. Thus driven into the arena of further oppression, like gladiators, they were forced to battle among themselves for a place of honor in the white establishment. So they hurt each other, and often they knew exactly why they were doing it.[3]

When Williams wrote his first novels in the late fifties and early sixties, he found himself facing the same one-black-writer-at-a-time syndrome in American letters. In spite of being a student of history and a devout believer in Wright's assessment of the difficult role of Blacks who write fiction especially, Williams persevered.

The author has Max complaining that "White writers were compared only to other white writers; black writers were compared only to other black writers" (167). Williams detailed this lament in an article he wrote in 1963.[4] There are also the homosexual publishers and critics with whom the writer must contend. In the novel effeminate Granville Bryant is called the Great White Father because he helps young black writers get started. Ironically, he also robs many of them of that dignity and manhood which Richard Wright/Harry Ames had said were so vital; for to cause a man to compromise himself sexually has to do irreparable harm in ways more than physical.

Now, Williams had attacked outright homosexual exploiters in *The Angry Ones,* but in *The Man Who Cried I Am* he includes a powerful symbol: Max's cancer of the anus. A grotesque symbol, indeed, the anal cancer represents on one level physical deterioration of the protagonist. On a broader plane, it represents the mortifying disease of mind and spirit to which the black man is susceptible. Whether a writer or not, he must endure a Sisyphean labor in any efforts to escape the pervasive putrefaction which blocks his progress toward integrity and self-pride. Some readers may feel that Williams went overboard in distastefulness with the cancer image. But, to be offended implies a consciousness, and to touch the reader's consciousness would be worth the attending discomfort. Further, the problem that the author is describing is no more appealing nor desirable to Blacks than cancer is. Sickness is not expected to appeal but to disgust. Williams hopes that along with the disgust may come efforts to find a remedy. With the eye of a medic, a perspective for which World War II could be thanked, he details Max's rotting and paining bowels throughout the novel. Another instance of Williams' turning to the grotesque to amplify racial injustice is the portraiture of Moses Boatwright in *The Man Who Cried I Am.*[5] Boatwright had been sentenced to death because of killing a white man and eating his genitals and heart. Prior to interviewing him, Max was a writer of cheery fiction and articles; after the interview Max would attempt to turn his writing into "a rumbling, threatening basso." Boatwright claims to have committed the cannibalistic act for four reasons: one, it was an enactment of what was expected of Blacks, who are supposed to be only slightly beyond barbarism; two, it demonstrated to what horrible lengths discrimination can drive a person; three, it offered Moses a chance to determine how he would die; and four, it gave him hope that his death might help better conditions. Says Moses,

" . . . I am an abomination. Ugly, black, cutting back on my thoughts so I wouldn't *embarrass* people, being superbly brilliant for the right people." (58)

Having to lead a robot-like existence, having to act dumb although he was a graduate of Harvard, and having, in fact, no control over his life, Boatwright commits an act which would give him some control, even if that control is just over the manner of death he dies. And his eating the heart and genitals rather than some other part of the corpse is because that is what life is all about, "clawing the heart and balls out of the other guy" (65).

Surely, Williams could have made his point about race prejudice and where it might lead without such a ghastly depiction of Boatwright, who has an orgasm each time he recounts his murder. His choice to use Boatwright, however, indicates his earnestness to employ the most naturalistic, bizarre and repulsive elements in his fiction to alert and disturb his readers about racial injustices. Williams does not blatantly insult the reader; rather he utilizes the Boatwright story and Max's cancer to shock and disgust first; then as the reader goes on, he finds himself almost unconsciously mulling over the implications of the two elements. At this point, the reader's initial shock gives way to a more calm reflection, and the chances are that Williams' denunciation of racism will make its mark. Notably, the author goes further than many novelists who merely shock for shock sake.

Another conflict to which Williams returns in *The Man Who Cried I Am* is the black man/white woman relationship. Steve and Lois in *The Angry Ones* bid their goodbyes when they become fed up with using each other. Keel and Della in *Night Song* bravely try to commit themselves to each other in spite of the problems they know must be overcome if they are to survive together. In fact, by the end of the novel Keel seriously considers marriage. Then, in *The Man Who Cried I Am* not only is Max married to a white woman but so is his co-protagonist, Harry Ames. Obviously, a progression can be traced from novel to novel; as if Williams were gradually grooming his characters to confront miscegenation. Along these same lines, it is worthwhile noting the various dispositions of the men in the stories. Steve has difficulty establishing his career because of prejudice which he finds almost overpowering. (It must be remembered that he had suicidal depressions.) So, when he decides to stand defiant, this means his standing ready to combat racism and with the help of his black sister-in-law, he hopes to have a better chance of success. But, not far from total despair, he is not about to consider marrying a white woman; the burden would be too great. Keel in *Night Song* has committed himself to rebellion some time ago. Secure in his belief that life is worth living if it can be lived the way one wants to, he turns away from the ministry toward which his parents had pushed him. Fortifying his rebellious spirit is the Olympian defiance of Eagle. Perhaps overconfidently, Keel falls in love with Della, only later to find himself so enraged by a society which would not tolerate his association that he becomes impotent. Max realizes how the media lures the black man toward "whitey Aphrodite, the love-and-sex object, raping it when he could, loving it when he was allowed to and marrying it when he dared to" (340). A mixed marriage, then, was the maximum revolt. It was an affirmation that one was a man in spite of color and that one was ready to publicly put oneself on the line to prove it. The mixed marriage testified that humans can and do fall in love, and Blacks, like Whites, are human. Now that his characters have the courage to make these affirmations, Williams diminishes the black man/white woman theme in his last two novels where his characters' primary concern becomes the thwarting of racist tendencies in America. Williams is saying that before the black man can fight racism on a large scale he must first conquer racism on an individual basis.

The irony of Max and Margrit's relationship is that it began and ended because Max wanted a surrogate for his black fiancee, Lillian Patch, who died while trying to abort Max's issue. He never forgave himself for being partly responsible for her death. In his quest to rectify his wrong, somehow, he welcomes Margrit, who seems a white reincarnation of black Lillian. Owing to brainwashing of massive proportions, the black man finds himself attracted at times to the white woman who appears as the forbidden fruit. The black woman has long tried to capture and imitate the style and appearance of the white woman (straightening her hair and wearing blond wigs, for example). The situation is reversed in Max and Margrit's relationship. Instead of a case in which the white woman is the ideal the black must copy, Lillian is the black ideal Margrit must live up to. The traditional roles of the women are reversed. Herein lies another example of how Williams uses a double-barrelled approach to his topics. First, he does complain outright about the white female mystique. Second, in the event that the reader might have overlooked or dismissed his complaint, he weaves it into the plot with subtle artistry. The theme, then, tends to have a more enduring effect than any sermonizing is likely to have.

Some favorite grievances of Williams also appear in *The Man Who Cried I Am*. He takes the offensive against those who feign a brotherhood to Blacks but betray them during crises. However, the Judas-figures are not only white like David Hillary in *Night Song;* they are black men who thrive on bringing about the demise of other Blacks. Before Max dies at the hands of black agents, he thinks:

> This is the final irony. The coming of age, Negro set at Negro in the name of God and Country. Or was it the ultimate trap? (401)

By making the traitors black, Williams affirms, as he tries to do in most of his novels, that there are two sides to the coin, that generalities and one-sided "truths" are not his idea of solving but of creating problems. This sense of fair play manifests itself throughout his works.

The author lashes out against clinging to security with the fervor found in books like *The Angry Ones* and *This Is My Country Too*. And, in eulogizing Lillian, Max praises the black mother, as Williams does in *Sissie,* while taking potshots at security and war:

Baby, didn't you understand? You over*whelmed* with your blackness, your babies; you choked them with the reek and tremor of the ghettoes they created; you screamed at their injustices which they denied because they must; you stacked up, created a backlog of book-hungry kids before the doors of their quota-oriented colleges, their Wall Street, communications centers, their theaters; you gave them political hacks, the ones who are worse liars and thieves than they, only to create a wedge through which the uncompromising can later pass; you produced good music for them to copy or steal—and you wrote more; you gave them your sons to help fight their wars (but that must stop—a dead Negro on a German, Japanese, French, American battlefield does very little for a live Negro pinioned to his ghetto). Out of all the garbage they leave for you, you produce, produce, produce, and scare the hell out of them, for if something can be made from garbage, why is it that they have only automobiles, Lillian? See what that desire for old American security got you, baby? Security. You are so goddamn secure now that you don't have to worry about where the next *any*thing is coming from. And God knows, you don't have to worry about me having a decent job so we can live the way you thought we ought to—according to their way, which is, my darling, as pitiable as it is, the only way now. (117)

The tone of this passage is one of tired frustration. Max has grown weary of being at the bottom rung of society. He sees Whites as being on top and Blacks at the bottom with life for Blacks generally being a constant battle for ascendancy to the level of Whites. "How did we get down here?" he asks. "We should have been out of here by now. Are we going to have to explode out" (117)? In the author's fifth novel the explosion would occur.

Some autobiographical items in *The Man Who Cried I Am* are Max's encounters with racism in the Army (though Williams was in the Navy) and the resolve of Max, while in the Army, to teach black soldiers how to survive foreshadows the actions of Abraham Blackman in *Captain Blackman*. Williams also treats the Prix de Rome fiasco through Harry Ames.[6] However, the author turns Ames' disappointment to triumph by having him befriended by a publisher, Kierzak, who advances Ames three thousand dollars on his work-in-progress and insists that he reject the thousand dollar consolation prize from the Lyceum. About the rejection, which apparently had racial undertones, Kierzak thinks:

> Everyone broke their balls looking for talent, but when they had it right in their semeny hands, it scared the crap out of them. (131-132)

One result of Williams' own rejection is that he would help establish *Amistad*, a journal devoted to the recognition and publication of black. writers with talent. No longer would a few Blacks, anyway, have to depend on the fickle and flimsy recognition of the white press and world.

Two facets of *The Man Who Cried I Am* have received such an abundance of attention that they distract the reader from other notable qualities in the novel. David Henderson, for instance, notes how Reverend Durell is a fictional version of Martin Luther King, Jr., Minister Q is Malcolm X, Max Reddick is Chester Himes, and as previously mentioned, Harry Ames is Richard Wright and Marion Dawes seems like James Baldwin.[7] All this is interesting enough but it doesn't take one very far. What it may do is send the reader on a hunting expedition to find what other characters may be linked to real-life figures. Chances are this expedition will divert one from important nuances to be found in the text. Furthermore, it must be remembered that no one character is a direct and consistent parallel of another person; that is, Max is not always Himes, Harry is not always Wright and so on. In fact, Richard Wright got to the heart of the matter when he said:

> The relationship between reality and the artistic image is not always direct and simple. The imaginative conception of a historical period will not be a carbon copy of reality. Image and emotion possess a logic of their own. A vulgarized simplicity constitutes the greatest danger in tracing the reciprocal interplay between the writer and his environment.[8]

Besides the search for historical parallels, immersing the King Alfred plan in historic contexts can also reap ambiguous results. On the positive side, the plan takes on greater significance: the Alliance Blanc, an international white organization, meets to consider means of dealing with a black/white race war which it sees as inevitable. Agencies of the U.S. government devise a contingency plan for the black threat in America. Their plan is named after King Alfred of England who had directed the translation of the *Anglo-Saxon Chronicle* and in that sense was a perpetuator of white history and, therefore, of white supremacy. Indeed, the strategy is to guarantee the perpetuation of the white race at the final expense of the black, "to terminate once and for all, the Minority threat to the whole of American society, and, indeed, the Free World" (372).

In the early sixties, the time of Max's discovery, concentration camps were still being kept in the U.S. as potential prisons for participants in any mass disruptions. No doubt, it was anticipated that the majority of the disruptors would be black. Hence, many black readers of *The Man Who Cried I Am* saw King Alfred as an affirmation of what was suspected all along. To add further coals to the fire, Williams has Max pass on the genocide plan to Minister Q who is subsequently killed by black agents to cover up government involvement. This encourages speculation on whether Malcolm X might have been assassinated, not because he defied Elijah Muhammed and the Nation of Islam, but because he had stumbled on some secret plot against Blacks.[9] So, the positive element of the meshing of fact and fiction is that it leaves the reader—particularly if he is black—temporarily incapable of separating the two, of delineating his emotional reaction to what is reported fact and to what is speculative fiction. This fusion may lend more immediacy and reality to Williams' ideas.

On the negative side, the plan, like some of the characters, distracts from the rest of the novel. The overall art of the novel tends to pale alongside the ending in which King Alfred is revealed in its entirety. Further, some readers may inadvertently find themselves responding to the novel as if it were a nonfiction treatise. Williams complains of the numerous people who expect him to confide in them the details of King Alfred or whatever plan he had uncovered. Maybe, though, this reaction does not have a totally negative import. For if Blacks may be made cautious and suspicious, they may be less vulnerable. And if the price for this defensive caution is that the art of *The Man Who Cried I Am* goes unnoticed, then Williams would definitely feel it a worthwhile loss for a much greater gain.

The handling of time in *The Man Who Cried I Am* is a further testimony to Williams' maturing artistry. As the novel opens Max is visiting his ex-wife after attending Harry's funeral. From this point to Max's own death takes less than seventy-two hours. But through a series of flashbacks, the rest of Max's life is filled in. The author had demonstrated a similar capability in dealing with time in *Sissie*. *The Man Who Cried I Am* is more complex, though, and the time scheme more intricate. The effect it has is that it makes the story seem amazingly short; only at the end of the text does one note that one has read over three hundred pages.

Among the varied subjects which the author explores is the question of where the black man is going. What must he do to insure his survival in a racist world? Other characters in the earlier novels had attempted to provide an answer. In *The Man Who Cried I Am,* Williams is more definitive, more gloomy than ever. The answers are two: recognize one's blackness and recognize who the enemy is. Max has an alter ego or inner voice, called Saminone, with which he exchanges quips.[10] Max insists that he was a man, that he was a writer, that he was someone important. The voice counters that he is black. In effect, his black side is his most important identity. It is not until the end after Max decides to give his life for the survival of his race that he begins to grasp somewhat the commitment that being black implies. And when the voice said "What you done was a black act," it is the highest compliment to be paid. On who the enemy is, Williams minces no words: "The enemy today is the believer in Anglo-Saxon updated racial mythology" (321). Black writers, like Ishmael Reed, would dedicate all their writings to deflating and leading Blacks away from that mythology.

Once, when Max is struggling to maintain integrity as a writer, he exclaims to white America: *"Give me my share! I am a man, Don't make me take it in this anger!"* This exclamation summarizes well what Williams emphasizes throughout *The Man Who Cried I Am.* Blacks want equality but prefer getting it peacefully. Yet, all signs indicate that this will not be the case. In his later novels, Williams would deal with frustrated Blacks who decided to take their share—in anger.

Notes To Chapter Five

1. John A. Williams, *The Man Who Cried I Am* (New York: Little, Brown & Co., 1967). Subsequent references will be to this edition.
2. _____, "Backtracking Pioneers," *New York Herald Tribune,* 7 June 1964.
3. _____, *The Most Native of Sons* (New York: Doubleday, 1970), p. 113.
4. _____, "The Literary Ghetto," *Saturday Review,* 20 April 1963, pp. 20, 40.
5. For an interesting account of Moses Boatwright, see Robert E. Fleming, "The Nightmare Level of *The Man Who Cried I Am,*" *Contemporary Literature,* Spring 1973.
6. See section on *Night Song* for details on Williams and the Prix de Rome award.
7. David Henderson, *"The Man Who Cried I Am:* A Critique," in *Black Expression,* ed. Addison Gayle, Jr. (New York: Weybright and Talley, 1969), pp. 365-371.
8. Richard Wright, "Blueprint for Negro Writing," in *The Black Aesthetic,* ed. Addison Gayle, Jr. (New York: Doubleday/Anchor Book, 1972), p. 325. Originally published in *New Challenge,* 1937.
9. Interestingly, in Williams' comparison of Minister Q and Reverend Durrell, he touches on a distinction which would be the crux of his preference of Malcolm X to Martin Luther King in *The King God Didn't Save.* In the following quote from *The Man Who Cried I Am,* all the reader need do is substitute King for Durrell and Malcolm X for Minister Q: "Where Durrell employed fanciful imagery and rhetoric, Minister Q preached the history, economics and religion of race relations; he preached a message so harsh it hurt to listen to it . . . Durrell's people came from the church-going middle class; Minister Q's from the muddiest backwashes of Negro life. The white man was going to have some choice to make between them, but he would, Max knew, choose to deal with the remembered image, and that would be Durrell." (209, 211)
10. Saminone is important because he constantly teases Max by calling him a "nigger," by playing the dozens with him and by attacking Max's hubris. Saminone keeps Max in touch with the reality that regardless of any personal successes he is still a black man and that there are the masses of Blacks who will never get his opportunities. Like old Professor Bazzam who emerges periodically through Europe, Saminone "reminds all the Negroes, who'd like to forget it, that they are, . . . He's like a bad penny or a conscience" (224-225).

Six

The Hymn of Return: Sons of Darkness, Sons of Light

Between *The Man Who Cried I Am* and *Sons of Darkness, Sons of Light* (1969)[1], John A. Williams witnessed ghetto riots and campus rebellions. He watched cities burn in reaction to Martin Luther King, Jr.'s assassination. And, the murder of Robert F. Kennedy dimmed the last hope of many Blacks of having a president who would be sensitive to their problems. On a more personal level, Williams had seen the praises of the critics over *The Man Who Cried I Am.* They were proclaiming him the most important black writer of the times. While some praised the novel for its interracial romances, others applauded its "blockbuster" ending. Very few seemed to give attention to all that the author was trying to say. Nevertheless, the book had catapulted Williams into a national prominence. But, there was little money accompanying this fame. So, for financial reasons he hurriedly wrote *Sons of Darkness, Sons of Light,* a novel which presents a race war in 1973.

Eugene Browning is a black, middle-aged, political science instructor who has left university life to become second-in-command of the Institute for Racial Justice. The IRJ is an NAACP-type organization with headquarters in New York City. Browning finds his hopes for racial equality sagging daily, and when a policeman shoots a black youth, he devises a plan for retaliation. *Sons of Darkness, Sons of Light,* therefore, presents the black man's response to the white treachery in *The Man Who Cried I Am.* Max Reddick had concluded that interracial conflict was inevitable. Browning not only recognizes the inevitability of the conflict but begins preparing himself for a role in that conflict. It is fitting, too, that the story takes place in the future. The author had described in past books what was to come if Whites did not respond to black cries for justice. In *Sons of Darkness, Sons of Light* the clash begins in 1973, the not-too-distant future from the vantage point of 1969.

Probably, because Williams had written his novel hurriedly and wanted to make it timely; it lacks the depth of *Sissie* or *The Man Who Cried I Am*. He treads old ground thematically, and the new subjects introduced do not receive a thorough investigation. Some of his pronouncements are remembered but without the force of those in some of his other writings. In effect, while *Sons of Darkness, Sons of Light* is not a bad novel, it is at best a mediocre one for Williams. The author himself appears to be experiencing the weariness, disgust and despair which he attributes to his characters. No wonder he begins turning, fictionally, to more desperate means to insure black survival. And if Browning's methods seem a little desperate, those of Abraham Blackman, one of Williams' future protagonists, will seem all the more frightening in their implications.

Whereas Williams had earlier dissected the atrocities of racism which would lead to a violent confrontation, in *Sons of Darkness, Sons of Light* he analyzes the mechanics of that confrontation. First, old methods such as boycotts and sit-ins will not work. Browning elaborates:

> . . . you had to obtain your goals by almost the same means *Chuck* obtained his, . . . and Chuck did not get his with Freedom Now or Love Your Brother marches. (11-12)

Second, unpremeditated violence will inevitably backfire. Dr. Millard Jessup, a leader of a guerrilla group which has its base in the California hills, intends to mobilize his black force at the slightest provocation. Browning thinks of him as being too militant:

> One could create the shock waves, that was easy, but it would not be easy to survive in the desolation of the murderous reaction; that had to come. The militants were like people who could not stand stitches, and so ripped them out, to their own detriment and everyone else's. (72)

Besides, Jessup's group consisted of too many people who "for all

110

their protestations believed in the status quo." One of his former henchmen criticizes his being too trusting of Blacks and Whites:

. . . he was trying to begin a black revolution with white money. And those cats Jessup's hanging out with have no plans for us except graves . . . He talks to too many people and too many people tend to guess and even know too much. The man's a fool; he still believes pure revolutionaries can come out of a system like this one, and he thinks that because a man's black he's an automatic revolutionary. Not true. (182)

So three taboos for a black revolt which might expect to stand some chance of success in America are thoughtless violence, an unguarded trust and an indiscreet broadcasting of intentions. The revolution of Eugene Browning and that of Trotman and Greene are likely to be more effective as they capitalize on Jessup's mistake.

Browning's idea is to have the policeman who had shot the black youth killed, hoping that it would indicate that Blacks were no longer going to accept brutality without equally brutal reactions. However, he plots to achieve his revenge anonymously through use of a Mafia killer, convinced that "power, real power, resided in anonymity."

The plan of Trotman and Greene, two disaffected followers of Jessup, is "to attack the system physically somewhere near the center of power. That is what would make the revolution a genuine revolution" (177). Specifically, they plant bombs at key bridges to New York City. By proving that they could cripple the largest city in the world, they hope to demonstrate their power. Then, their demands would be presented to the government. They would insist on mass resignations of racist government officials, allocation of land to Blacks, higher pay for professional workers, and a civilian police review board.

But even the strategies of retaliation and massive disruption have their weak points. After Browning has the cop killed, policemen retaliate by killing three black students which in turn leads to a mushrooming round of revenge between black and white. Browning realizes that although his immediate aim is fulfilled, he has sparked violence of greater proportions than he anticipated.

The simple, selective violent act, calculated to deliver a message, had become magnified. All the black populace he had been trying to save from slaughter looked like it was being slaughtered after all. (269)

Trotman and Greene effect the dynamiting of bridges, but only at the expense of losing trust in each other. Suspecting Trotman of duplicity Greene locks him in a closet while the bombing takes place. Greene wonders,

What in the hell was it all for if it soured you on brothers? Or soured them on you? What kind of insanity lurked behind the attempts to alter an already insane society that had indicated that insanity was at its very core? (240)

As the novel ends, New York City is in panic and the war between the races has spread nationally. How it all will end, the author does not say. The implication is, though, that he expects a return to normalcy, which means a return to a racist society; for he has Browning resolve to return to teaching: "I won't teach the way I taught before," he says. "I'm going to teach down this system, if I can, . . ." (258). With this determination, the novel has come almost full circle, from a disenchantment with working within the precepts of society to a violent revolution and back to rebellion within the system. One can guess it will not be too long before people like Browning despair once more. Then there might be no turning back.

Sons of Darkness, Sons of Light is subtitled, "A Novel of Some Probability." What Williams describes is indeed probable, and the book may serve the dual purpose of warning Whites of what may be imminent if black/white relations are not improved as well as warning Blacks of the pitfalls of which they must beware if they decide to rebel. As a propagandist tract the novel succeeds marginally. Still it could have been more successful as a novel had its subject been handled more subtly. As is, the directness of Williams' message shocks, but for too short a time.

However, *Sons of Darkness, Sons of Light* does contain some interesting observations. First, rebellion is likely to begin with the middle class. Trotman, Greene and Browning are all middle-aged, middle-class people. They have simply reached the limits of their endurance. Unlike the masses who can gain release from shouting, demonstrating and showing the black-power sign, these men see that little progress is being made in spite of those exhibitions. In fact, society seems to move along as if the dissidents were not there. Having the perspective of an onlooker, and an overwhelming hatred of their own immobility, the middle class is ripe for revolution. In a time when the middle class is projected as the passive enemy, it is worthwhile to remember that it may very well turn out to be a sleeping giant.

A second insight can be found in the depiction of Bill Barton, director of the Institute for Racial Justice. When the police suspect that Greene had killed a policeman, Barton suddenly sees his chance: find Greene's whereabouts, turn him in, collect the reward and use it "to continue on a full budget and help hundreds." Certainly, the author views this type of behavior as a black betrayal symbolic of real life sellouts in less dramatic situations. In *The King God Didn't Save,* Williams complains further against black sellout by civil rights leaders. The sad fact is that the sellout does occur.

A discussion between Browning and a Mafia Don reveals a third insight: the misconception that intellectuality and violence are heterogeneous ideas. Browning agrees with the Don that

" . . . Intelligence doesn't have anything to do with how much a man can take. It can help him rationalize away the use of violence, thinking about his own skin, but that same intelligence will tell him, finally, that he's got no choice but to be as tough as the next guy or tougher." (192)

This position refutes Greene's impression that because Browning was a college professor, he was ignorant of racism and the aggressive recoil it provoked. Perhaps Williams included this discussion for the benefit of black college students and graduates who may lapse into inactivity and a false security.

Ronald Walcott says of Williams' fiction:

Inevitably in the throes of dissolution, marriage is the personal drama of his characters as the temptation of violence is their political drama.[2]

113

Typically, there is a marital conflict in *Sons of Darkness, Sons of Light* between Browning and his wife Valerie. Black and accustomed to a middle-class existence, Valerie nags Browning for spending so much time with the IRJ while paying little attention to their teenage daughter who is dating a white youth. Browning repeats a complaint which most of Williams' protagonists echo at one time or another:

I look and listen and you've become, night by night, deed by deed, just like the others. You don't dream any more and perhaps you never did. (9)

The relationship does not have a chance of survival until Browning, disillusioned after putting so much faith in his plan of revolt, decides to put some faith in another human being as well. Similarly, Val does not accept her daughter's dating a White until she herself is caught in adultery by her husband. Then, she sees the folly of her pretentious superiority to her daughter's white boyfriend. Then she can shake his hand in an acknowledgement that they are both of the same frail and human stock. Interestingly, Val learns a lesson which all the killings could not teach the other characters in the novel.

Consistent with his sense of balance and fair play, Williams introduces the Jewish freedom struggle through Itzhak Hod, an Israeli refugee in America and a professional killer for the Mafia. Rather touching is his effort to understand why Blacks have waited so long to rebel.

Many of the reviews of *Sons of Darkness, Sons of Light* pinpoint its weaknesses. Says one reviewer:

It raises, by inference, many profound moral questions. It relates the bitter counterpoint of black humiliation and suffering with the long suffering of Jews. It conjures up the nightmare arising from the stupid and hypocritical values of a society living by traditions and ambivalences. But it does not explore any of these questions with the powerful insights that are imperative. It rests its case too soon and too superficially.[3]

Another writes:

But a novel that winds up so many themes and characters cannot put them all to rest in 279 pages. The characters bustle but do not grow in complexity. Nor does the background fill up: the performers always seem to be the only people in New York that day. John Williams has a notable, attractive author's voice and an impressive range of sympathy, but this time he has been content to do a skin job.[4]

Unquestionably, the novel does end abruptly. Williams has Browning copulating while a race war rages in the background. This setting may amuse or irritate the reader. In any event, it makes Browning look as if he has abandoned the struggle when he is most needed—even if there is very little that he can do. It is also likely that the ending in bed of a revolution that began in the streets may seem anticlimatic, to say the least.

One reason the plot of *Sons of Darkness, Sons of Light* closes so inconclusively may be that the author was not too convinced of the workability of his plan for revolution. In the case of Browning and in that of Trotman and Greene , the cataclysmic act was performed, but where would it end? Perhaps Williams had overhurried in presenting his criticism of the various methods he sees being advanced by groups such as the Black Panther Party—which in baldest terms is what *Sons of Darkness, Sons of Light* is all about. However, his plan is tentative. In *Captain Blackman* he advances another.

Notes to Chapter Six

1. John A. Williams, *Sons of Darkness, Sons of Light* (New York: Little, Brown & Co., 1969). Subsequent references will be to this edition.
2. Ronald Walcott, "*The Man Who Cried I Am*: Crying in the Dark," *Studies in Black Literature*, 3, No. 1, (1972) p. 30.
3. Henrietta Buckmaster, "He Gives Anger Definition," *Christian Science Monitor* 7 August 1969, p. 7.
4. Wilfred Sheed, "Race War Novel, with a Cast of Thousands," *Book World* 29 June 1969, p. 5.

Seven

Uncle Sam's Gratitude: Captain Blackman

Captain Blackman (1972)[1] begins with the wounding of Abraham Blackman in Viet Nam. While he is unconscious, the novel relates as in a dream the roles of Blacks in battles and wars from the Revolutionary Wars of 1776 to Viet Nam. The inclusion of heavily documented but not much publicized materials helps to bring to light the unsung heroisms of Black soldiers during the last two centuries. Still, for all their sacrifices, they were denied full citizenship because of their skin color.

It would not be an exaggeration to say that John A. Williams had been preparing for Captain Blackman since his discharge from the Navy in 1946. He had been disappointed and disillusioned by his experiences in the service. The racist treatment the author received was extremely traumatic. No wonder he tried to expose the racism in the Armed Forces in his fiction and nonfiction. To illustrate, one of the first novels he wrote was *The Cool Ones* which was never published. The story is about three black youths, Johnny and Orrin, who enter the Navy, and Davis, who goes into the Army; all face discrimination in their various units. Williams rewrote *The Cool Ones* several times and if he had his choice, it, instead of *The Angry Ones,* would have been his first published novel. In *The Angry Ones*, Steve Hill bitterly recalls the irony of his brother who died fighting for a country where his wife and children could barely survive. In the same year (1960) *The Angry Ones* was released, Williams began another novel, called *Moody's Squad.* An unfinished text, it is the story of Gideon Moody, who is a forerunner of Abraham Blackman in physique and background; that is, he has a Herculean stature and has

117

come to the Army seeking refuge from the ghetto. Moody reflects on the dilemma of

> Colored troops. And as soon as he thought that he knew that sometime in the future, when the war was over, the glory of having shared it would be empty, for of what value were colored troops in the final essence anyway?[2]

In *Sissie,* when Ralph's younger brother is killed in Korea, Ralph comprehends the dilemma verbalized by Moody. Without a fictional cloak, Williams complains outright in *This Is My Country Too*. It is there that he tells of his own mistreatment in the Navy. In *The Man Who Cried I Am,* Max Reddick resolves to teach his black troop the facts about army life; while in *Sons of Darkness, Sons of Light,* one character feels that the only good the Armed Forces serve is to give Blacks an insight into war tactics that could be used against white America. Lastly, in *The King God Didn't Save,* Williams chides Martin Luther King, Jr. for being too distant from the black misery. But when King turned his attention to Viet Nam, to the Blacks and Vietnamese who were both being victimized, the author lauded him for finally attacking a problem relevant to most black males in America.

In 1966, Williams had taken *The Angry Black,* removed his own short stories and those by Ralph Ellison, added pieces like G. C. Oden's "Man white, brown girl and all that jazz"; Gwendolyn Brooks' poem "Medgar Evers"; and "Navy black" a story from his own novel in progress. ("Navy black" was subsequently abandoned.) What resulted was *Beyond the Angry Black.*[3] The plot of "Navy black" revolves around a base with black sailors on Guam during World War II. A black cook finds his plans to adopt a Chamarro youth frustrated by the youth's discovery of the racism which awaits him in the U.S. While this drama occurs on the individual level, it contrasts with a general jubilation of the men who anticipate an end to the war. More complex than "Son in the Afternoon," "Navy black" testifies to Williams' skill in capturing wartime life. It provides one further documentation to the continuing interest of the author in depicting racial strife in the service.

After the publication of *The King God Didn't Save* and *The Most Native of Sons* in 1970, Williams turned his attention to some information he had collected on discrimination at bases in different parts of the country. At long last it seemed that he would be able to write a full-length book on atrocities too readily overlooked. Besides, he was an accepted black writer and would not have the difficulties getting a book published as he had when he wrote *The Cool Ones* in 1957. He petitioned the State Department for permission to visit with black soldiers stationed in Southeast Asia, since it was in Viet Nam, Cambodia and Laos that so many Americans had died, of whom a suspicious proportion had been black. Obviously, the two decades since World War II had wrought little change of attitudes toward the black soldier. However, Williams could not raise enough monetary support for the trip. He would have to publish his book without some of the information he wanted; and since he was not satisfied presenting what he had in a nonfictional form, he decided to deliver his material in a novel. The result was *Captain Blackman*.

The form of *Captain Blackman* is intriguing. As previously noted, the movement through history occurs as if in Blackman's dream. Although Williams does not try to maintain this impression, he does suggest a plausible rationale: Abraham Blackman teaches a black military history seminar in which he outlines to his black class how history stands against them. Hence, they have no reason to be heroes in wartime only to return to being villains in peacetime. He illustrates his position by teaching about Blacks during the American Revolution, the War of 1812, the Civil War, the Plains Wars, the Spanish-American War, World War I, The Spanish Civil War, World War II, the Korean War, and ultimately Viet Nam. His one lesson is this:

We don't have anything to prove to anybody, . . . We've done it over and over and over again. No heroes. Just do your jobs. (15)

When Blackman spends hours unconscious in a hospital, it is not unusual that he would dream about what he teaches: the various wars in which Blacks have participated over and over again without equity, much less recognition or reparation.

The passages through time are interspersed with returns to the present. At one point when the narrator switches to the present, it turns out that Blackman has been unconscious for only a minute, yet he has relived three major wars during that period. So the present time of the story covers but a few days, and the author crowds the history of generations into those days. Because the movement in the past as well as the switch from past to present are so subtle, the novel creates a surrealistic effect. Time becomes fluid; past and present seem to merge. This technique helps to illustrate the author's thesis that little difference exists between past history and present as far as treatment of the black man is concerned.

Throughout the text are sections called "Cadences" and "Drumtaps." The Cadences usually consist of conversation between historical figures. For example, interchange between white bigoted officers are recorded at conference tables as they seal the fate of Blacks on the battlefield. Drumtaps include written communications from Presidents and famous Generals. These two sections expose directly the racism of prestigious leaders like Abraham Lincoln and Theodore Roosevelt. Many of the revelations may be hard to believe and the reader may begin to wonder where Williams got his information. Most of the historical material he researched himself, but books have been published in the last decade to which the reader can go to verify his accuracy.[4] For instance, many startling, racist comments which the author attributes to American presidents are supported by George Sinkler in *The Racial Attitudes of American Presidents*.[5] The presence of so much historical data often obscures the distinction between fact and fiction.

On a broad scale, Williams succeeds in making two points about history: it is a snare in which the Black will remain entrapped unless he can learn from that history. Also, because the pattern of history is cyclic, it is inevitable that the white man will have to reckon with the black. When Blackman first begins to dream, he appears during the Revolutionary War with his twentieth century memory; that is, he is still aware of all that will happen during that and future wars. It is not long, though, before he merges with the times and loses his consciousness of other events and of the times from which he came. In this, he typifies Blacks being caught up in their immediate history; whereas a broader historical perspective is necessary for progress. Forecasting the acquiring of this perspective plus a turnabout for the white oppressors, Blackman thinks:

We're all trapped by our history; playing games, doing the easiest and the most obvious, but one day that'll change and it'll be terrible to see. (54)

As the reader may easily gather, Abraham Blackman stands as an allegorical figure for the black American serviceman throughout the centuries. To underscore the minimal recognition the black serviceman has made, Williams has Blackman begin as a private in the Revolutionary War; it is not until the present that he is promoted to Major, and this occurs mainly because he has been maimed in battle. Williams suggests that it has taken the black man all these years to rise through the military ranks, and still top posts are denied him.

As Abraham of the Old Testament was the founder of the Hebrew people, so is Abraham Blackman the founder of a new breed of Blacks who will insure the survival of the race. Major Ishmael Whittman, Blackman's nemesis, represents the white man as outcast, an historical anachronism fighting futilely to maintain the white supremacy held in the past. The antagonism of Blackman and Whittman exists on an allegorical and realistic level. Within the fictional realm Whittman had been beaten by Blackman in a personal skirmish during the Korean War. Now that Blackman lies injured in Viet Nam, Whittman delights in the injury. Ultimately, Blackman engineers the demise of Whittman by capitalizing on his racial prejudice.

Perhaps the most fascinating character in the novel besides Captain Blackman is his female counterpart, Mimosa Rodgers. She is the prototypic black woman who, like Blackman, has survived the abuses of the centuries: "Mimosa" is the name of a touch-me-not plant which folds its leaves when it is touched but opens out again shortly thereafter. Like the plant, Mimosa Rodgers is irrepressible. Her hardships correspond to the plant being touched; her survival equals the inevitable opening of the plant.

When first seen in history, Mimosa is a slave-girl during the Civil War. White men have raped her, but Blackman avenges her. Next, she is a student at Drake University and a product of the Reconstruction era. Then, she appears as the wife of a pilot during World War II. Lastly, she is a foreign service officer with immense influence in Viet Nam. In spite of hardships throughout history, the black woman, represented by Mimosa, has endured. Finally, Williams seems to be saying, she is being acknowledged by the world (Mimosa in the present is not a maid or teacher—the traditional roles of black women; instead she works in the foreign office in Saigon). Yet her position is not ideal. She still has to give the black man moral support lest he falter and quit. Mimosa understands only too well how Blackman's loss of a leg (the result of being hit in Viet Nam) may threaten his feeling of manhood, and she provides him with courage to live and to fight racism.

An interesting metamorphosis of Mimosa occurs. As a slave girl, she is described as thin and small. As a present-day member of the foreign office, she is described as big in stature, complementing the hugeness of Captain Blackman. Obviously this physical growth symbolizes a social and psychical progress.

Two other noteworthy characters are Doctorow and Woodcock. Doctorow is a Jew whom Blackman enlightens about racism. They become compatriots. After the war Doctorow plans to write a book detailing racial discrimination in the Armed Forces. His kinship with Blackman seems to reflect the author's view that Blacks and Jews can be a mutual help to each other. Woodcock is a light-skinned black who could pass for white were it not for his Afro. He is dubbed Newblack by Blackman since men of Woodcock's complexion could be the key to the success of the black revolution.

Intermingled with these characters who with varied significance move through history are the monstrous atrocities of the wars—the slaughter of black prisoners during the Civil War, the dishonorable discharge of one hundred and sixty-six black soldiers at Brownsville, Texas in 1906,[6] and the Tombolo massacre during World War II. A powerful and moving scene occurs between the black man and the Indian during the Plains War. The Indians want to know how the Blacks who are oppressed by Whites can join the Whites to oppress Indians. Guiltily, Captain Blackman replies that he is following orders. The Indians respond that the time will come when Blacks will be willing to fight and die for freedom, just as they, the first Americans, were doing then.

Williams manages to get one of his frequently used topics, security, into *Captain Blackman*. Observing how the armies of the past and present attract Blacks because they symbolize hope and stability (Blackman saw a military career as a refuge from ghetto life), the narrator explains that in this case more than any other, the quest for security becomes "the killing search."

In the last chapter of *Captain Blackman*, a black strategy is effected which would cripple the U.S. It entails having all Blacks who could pass for white do so in order to get jobs at nuclear stations in defense operations. As the book ends, Woodcock a *passe blanc* assists his white commander—who not unexpectedly is Whittman—by extending a helping hand as he boards a plane. Like Prufrock's snickering footman, Woodcock knows he has finally fathomed Whittman's weakness. The flaw of Whittman, and of the white man in general, is that he is a slave to appearances. He had trusted men because of their color. Now this same specious basis was being made to backfire. Thousands of fair-skinned Blacks disguised as Whites had engineered a conflict between the U.S. and Russia. As the Russian missiles are about to fall on the nation, Whittman realizes the black trickery and says in shock, "Woodcock didn't *look* colored."

The switch from the semi-historical accounts to the fantastic, yet plausible, takeover in the last chapter runs the risk of jolting the reader too much, although he has been prepared for a revolution. This jolt is probably inevitable in any quick move from the actual to the probable. It may be, though, that this was exactly the effect Williams wanted to create. After all, there is nothing calming about the possibility of having to destroy one's country before it destroys one.

All in all, the fusion of allegorical characters, fictional, historical and documentary materials, a fluid time scheme and a plan for the overthrow of racist America—the fusion of all these diverse elements qualifies *Captain Blackman* as the most ambitious and experimental effort of the author. A historical novel in the vein of Arna Bontemps' *Black Thunder* and Robert Graves' *I, Claudius,* it conveys its history in a reportorial style. The journalistic training of the author shows here as never before. Through expert and controlled handling of both fiction and history, he fulfills his own criterion for a historical novel:

> A novelist embarked on a historical work becomes a historian in effect, and he must evaluate his character in terms of the time in which his character lived. He is required to be *both* a novelist and a historian.[7]

One critic complains that while the handling of the history is done well, the fictional techniques seem cumbersome and intrusive."[8] On the whole, however, critical response to *Captain Blackman* has been guarded, taking a wait-and-see attitude. Few reviewers, however, do commit themselves. For instance, one writer says about the book that "Williams is too good a novelist to be writing tracts."[9] Another conjectures that the novel "may turn out to be among the most important works of fiction of the decade."[10]

Whatever the response to *Captain Blackman*, it seems a fitting close to the study of Williams' fiction. His first novel, *The Angry Ones*, includes his own history. *Captain Blackman* incorporates a major portion of the black man's history. If the movement of a fiction writer away from himself is any indication of his maturity, then Williams has come a long way during his twelve years of publishing novels.

Notes To Chapter Seven

1. John A. Williams, *Captain Blackman* (New York: Doubleday & Co., 1972).
2. To be found in the John A. Williams Collection in the George Arents Research Library for Special Collections at Syracuse University.
3. Williams, ed., *Beyond the Angry Black* (New York: Cooper Square Publishers, 1966).
4. See books like Benjamin Quarles' *The Negro in the Civil War* and *The Negro in the Making of America;* Herbert Aptheker's *American Negro Slave Revolts;* and Thomas Higgins' *Black Rebellion.*
5. George Sinkler, *The Racial Attitudes of American Presidents* (New York: Anchor Books, 1972).
6. Only recently has the Army changed its position on the Brownsville disruption and awarded posthumously honorable discharges to the black soldiers.
7. John A. Williams, "The Manipulation of History and of Fact: An Ex-Southerner's Apologist Tract for Slavery and the Life of Nat Turner; or William Styron's Faked Confession" in *William Styron's Nat Turner: Ten Black Writers Respond*, ed. John Henrik Clarke (Boston: Beacon Press, 1968), p. 46.
8. Leonard Fleischer, rev. of *Captain Blackman*, by John A. Williams, *Saturday Review*, 13 May 1972, p. 86.
9. Eric Moon, rev. of *Captain Blackman*, by John A. Williams, *Library Journal*, 1 May 1972, p. 1742.
10. George Davis, "A Revolutionary War Soldier in Vietnam," *The New York Times Book Review*, 21 May 1972, p. 14.

Eight

Conclusion

To delight and instruct are the immemorial ends of literature. The first Chaucer termed the chaff, the second the fruit. Aestheticians have quarrelled endlessly over which should be given primacy. But the artifact that well achieves both should be, theoretically at any rate, irreproachable. This theory evidently has basis in fact since literary masterpieces of the ages have catered to the moral and pleasure impulses of man. Form and technique, in the meantime, must be functional, not tangential, otherwise they distract from rather than facilitate the achievement of the twin goals.

In a century that included two World Wars, the ascendancy of Communism, the unleashed forces of capitalism and industrial technology, the vacillations between economic depression and inflation, the existence of a Cold War between Russia and America, and the emergence of the People's Republic of China as a third power to reckon with—in such a time when so much appalls, threatens and dwarfs the individual to self-destruction and insanity, how can one expect the writer to produce humorous little ditties? Yet the need to elevate oneself from the mire has been overpowering. In one instance, therefore, there appears the gloom of a *1984, The Stranger, City of Night, Cast the First Stone, The Rainbow,* and *Absalom, Absalom.* In another, there is an abundance of the so-called escapist literature, some of it labeled science-fiction, others westerns and love stories. This second type skirts social problems of today and humors the reader with imaginary worlds as far removed from reality as possible. Since these stories serve as a therapeutic release, they should not be overly criticized. However, the reader who rushes to these writings and refuses to deal with their antitheses deserves severe criticism. One need only look at the Best Sellers list to get an idea of what kind of literature Americans are reading today. The inclination toward writing that does not disturb or provoke sobriety is partly the faults of the writers and the readers but, as indicated earlier, it is mostly the result of a country that refuses to face up to its many ills, a country that will insist in the midst of gross moral decay and corruption that it is the seat of divine infallibility.

An American writer like John A. Williams surfaces as one of few in the present field who remains dedicated to disseminating the truth rather than writing around it. As a member of an incalculably maligned race, he has as much a vested interest in truth—historical truth, especially—as the oppressor of his race has in perpetuating lies. He said in 1964:

> In America the novelist is only just beginning to correct history. Is it because the losers who have joined their ranks have made them aware of gross manipulation of it or is it because of the losers outside their ranks? In either case, we have viewed history poorly illustrated for too long. The illustrations have been altered, sections have been omitted, and mythographers have filled in the gaps.
>
> I am now talking about American history as it has illustrated the Negro and as it has affected this nation for generations. Dismiss it, if you will, but then dismiss American history altogether.[1]

So the obligation of the writer to history is paramount, and the novels of Williams illustrate his meeting this obligation. Richard Wright once wrote:

> Theme for Negro writers will emerge when they have begun to feel the meaning of the history of their race as though they in one lifetime had lived it themselves throughout all the long centuries.[2]

As a matter of fact, Williams follows verbatim this pattern for a theme in *Captain Blackman*. But a concern for the history of the black man does not necessarily imply a retreat from the universal:

> . . .I don't think because a Negro writes about Negroes he does not write on a larger scale. First you are a human being, then a writer. . . .[3]

126

The fiction and nonfiction qualify the author as a vanguard in American letters. *The Angry Ones,* although falling closest to what has been described, with undue derogatory import, as formula protest fiction has nevertheless transcended that mold by incorporating tremendous insights and a sense of fair play. In regard to the latter, the novel does not scream bloody murder for Blacks alone but for the non-Blacks as well who suffer mistreatment. *Africa: Her History, Lands and People* demonstrates an interest in the black mother country long before having such an interest was fashionable, and just as it punctured myths about Africa so would *This Is My Country Too* expose America with a skill and forthrightness that surpasses its predecessor, *Travels with Charley. Night Song* translates with precision a white refugee's stay in a world of black musicians into a mythic journey to the underworld. Some of the characters achieve epic proportions, which only heightens the tragedy when the arrows pierce the vulnerable heels. *Sissie* departs from the sweet and syrupy tale of the black matriarch; the author remains true to this end until the last line of the book. In *Sissie* one can see a handling of time that diverges from the previous novels; one can note a certain ease in managing a difficult subject. And from the standpoint of style and subject matter, one may be able to understand why *Sissie* is the best fiction, all in all, by the writer.

While white publishers were beginning to respond to black unrest by printing practically anything concerning Blacks, no matter how trashy, *The Man Who Cried I Am* represented a breath of fresh air. It was a story of contemporary interest, stirring to restlessness those who were afraid to think how plausible the King Alfred Plan might be. Sadly, Samuel Yette's *The Choice* afforded no relief a few years later when it documented much of what Williams had presented fictionally. The form of *The Man Who Cried I Am* probably never will be fully appreciated as it may be forgotten in the aftermath of the horrifying conclusion. Yet, a technical maturation evidences itself therein. *Sons of Darkness, Sons of Light* might have been considered a better book if the reader were unaware of the author's capabilities. Thematically, however, it is right on course as it faces the possibility and ramifications of a race war, coming to practical conclusions akin to those found in *Imperium in Imperio, Black Thunder* and *The Spook Who Sat by the Door.* Surely, if there is one area in which Blacks cannot afford to be impractical, it is that of guerrilla warfare against white America.

127

The King God Didn't Save dared register unfavorable commentary on a giant civil rights leader at a time when everyone was still paying *pro forma* homage. Numerous black authors have since criticized King, some more severely than Williams, but he was the first to hazard recording his impressions whatever their unpopularity. *The Most Native of Sons* has celebrated one of the best novelists of the century. *Captain Blackman* can teach its readers more about the role Blacks played in American wars than most history books. Finally, *Flashbacks* proves that the author is no superman but suffers the same hurts, joys and disappointments as anybody else.

Returning to the age-old purposes of literature, the writings of Williams entertain in places but never, never do they resort to entertainment at the expense of the truth. And this quest for truth infuses the works with a high moral and instructional value. About technique and form, the author is also unequivocal. The twofold duties of the black writer must be 1) "to become an educator, a teacher, a story-teller, a satirist, any vehicle that will help make his people aware of their positions" and 2) "to become an expert in his craft."[4] The message is all-important, he says, and a faulty craft distorts the message. Blacks must not merely be satisfied with writing good novels but

. . .to the extent that the American novel has thus far served us so poorly in terms of how we appear in them as they're written by Whites, we really ought to try to experiment with the novel form. Turn it around. Find something else that we can do either to advance it so that it becomes a better vehicle for our message or to make it so that a novel written by Norman Mailer will be so outdated that he'll have to sit down and write like us.[5]

A dedication to excellence on so many fronts is what makes Williams a giant in his field.

When the question arises about what the province of the black novelist should be, the answer from Williams' example is the human condition, and one cannot treat the condition of man in America without touching on man's injustices to his fellowman, which will be interracial and intraracial. The delineations of these injustices are endless, and herein lies a hint as to what Williams himself will be doing in upcoming books. He will explore human injustice from vantage points too frequently ignored. Specifically he intends to incorporate into future novels prehistorical and anthropological studies which open a whole different avenue of questions about the traditional roles of black peoples to white. How long will he continue in championing the cause of equality among man, particularly here in the United States? Chester Himes says,

It is a long way, a hard way from the hatred of the faces to the hatred of evil, a longer way still to the brotherhood of men.[6]

Until this long road to brotherhood shortens, Williams sees himself committed to his subject matter. But as Himes also says, growth must attend this commitment. And if growth is "the surviving influence in our lives,"[7] then John A. Williams would have already contributed his share of the growth of many should he not write another word.

*   *   *

This study has tried to bring to light the development of an artist who because he is black faces the burden of race along with those incumbent upon any serious artist. Anticipating that many who approach this study will not have read all of John A. Williams' works, more time goes to elaborating plots than might otherwise be the case. Lastly, the ultimate hope is that this study will provoke others to conduct investigations of their own not just into books by Williams but those by the numerous other black writers who have received little more than fleeting, patronizing attention from critics.

Notes To Chapter Eight

1. John A. Williams, "Backtracking Pioneers," *New York Herald Tribune*, 7 June 1964
2. Richard Wright, "Blueprint for Negro Writing," in *The Black Aesthetic,* ed. Addison Gayle, Jr. (New York: Doubleday/Anchor, 1972), p. 324.
3. Williams, "An Author Integrates," *Chicago Daily News*, 18 May 1963.
4. See the Appendix of this study.
5. *Ibid*.
6. Chester Himes, "Dilemma of the Negro Novelist in the U.S.," in *Beyond the Angry Black*, ed. John A. Williams (New York: Mentor, 1971), p. 80.
7. *Ibid*.

Nine

Appendix

i

Interview—October 25, 1971

(My first meeting with novelist John A. Williams was on October 25, 1971, when he came to give a reading at the University of New Mexico. We had corresponded previously and had planned to have further discussions on his arrival. A small man with thin, receding hair and with what he calls a mephistophelean beard, Williams exhibited an infectious warmth and affableness which immediately helped one to feel comfortable in his presence. Still under the impression that writers tend to have quirks, I became more amazed as I discerned that Mr. Williams appeared to have no obvious eccentricities. In fact there was little, externally, to distinguish him as a writer.

For approximately three hours, we talked—mostly, he answered my questions on his writings, his political opinions, his concerns and expectations for American Blacks. Williams' candor which permeates his nonfiction can be found as well in the following transcript of my interview with him. Where some authors might have hedged, he was unequivocal without giving the impression of being foolhardy or pompous.

The interviews (there would be a second in the summer of 1972) may appear slightly dated, but they confirm ideas and beliefs which have been presented in the works of the writer. Moreover, the reader will get a picture of a man calling attention to history and all its lessons. If a desperation emerges, it is precisely because Williams feels that man is generally too indifferent to past and present events and their effect on what is to come.)

CASH: You seemed to be fascinated with the black musician's world. What influenced that?

WILLIAMS: Well, I think if we hadn't been poor, I would have been a musician. When I was a kid, I was in a drum and bugle corps and I was a good bugler. I wanted to study trumpet, but as cheap as it was to study trumpet at that time and to rent one—my folks didn't have the money, so I just stayed a good bugler, and that was it. The strange thing is that my boy did study trumpet, and he is a good trumpeter.

CASH: So, you didn't have any humanitarian purposes in *Night Song* like recording for posterity or for the readers a more in-depth insight into the black musician and perhaps the role played or what his role was all about?

WILLIAMS: I don't think I set out to do that consciously. God knows I know enough musicians to know what they were going through, what they do go through.

There's something else that struck me lately. In *The Angry Ones* and in *Night Song,* you've got this tandem pair of black guys Keel and Eagle and Obie and Steve. You've got the same thing in *The Man Who Cried I Am.* Now early I was very aware that this was the only way to deal with black dialogue; that is, to have another confidant. Or as in the case of *The Man Who Cried I Am,* Harry is not always a confidant. He is an antagonist. But at least they can dialogue. And to a larger extent having two characters function like this, you're really dealing with one character, but using two parts.

CASH: I see what you mean. I suppose that's why Obie complements Steve Hill by giving his commentary every so often. Speaking about dialogue, I note that in many of the novels the characters are black and educated. If you have a black educated man, he is likely not to speak the slang or use the terminology of the masses. Do you find that dialogue easier to deal with than if you were to work with a less educated group? Is there any expediency in one as opposed to the other?

WILLIAMS: Again I have to deal out of my own experiences. As a matter of fact, one of the novels I'm working on now, the one that encompasses the guys from all classes, several of the characters are skilled workers. They've not gone to school or anything. The peculiar thing about a place like Syracuse is whether you've gone to college or not, everybody's language is approximately the same. We notice differences, say, in people who come up from the South. Because their language is different doesn't mean they're lower class. Even before they came there we had lower-class people who spoke as well as any preacher who got up on the pulpit. Maybe it's just the difference of location, New York State vs. Mississippi or whatever, and the kinds of education that people got. It's something I really hadn't thought about until you just brought it up, but it's really remarkable.

CASH: I think whether we like it or not, language is one of the means of stereotype. So if you're speaking what might be called the black dialogue, people associate you immediately with the low class. And if you speak standard English, they associate you immediately with the middle class, which is ridiculous and can really throw people off base. It's like anything else. You have a suit on, you're well-shaved and some Whites are prone to give you nice comments. On the other hand, if you are looking grubby, they'll hardly acknowledge your existence.

WILLIAMS: In this new book, there's a guy who's a pusher. Two or three guys work in the foundry. Yet, the language really isn't that different from the guys who grew up, went to college, moved away and who are now coming back. I mean, to talk to my father,—who lives in Syracuse and has re-married, as has my mother—to talk to my father man-to-man without any concern for certain fine points of grammar, he talks just like me. There are certain things he does once in a while with his verbs and pronouns, but, hell, I heard that even Robert Graves does that.

CASH: This brings me to another question which arises because you do deal with Blacks who have a college education and many who have gone beyond that in their own readings and experiences. Let's take Eugene Browning in *Sons of Darkness, Sons of Light*. There are perhaps many reasons why his revolutionary idea, his salvific act, doesn't work. History in itself would have shown him it wasn't going to. But, he was a professor, a teacher, who decides to get into the action. So, he joins the IRJ, I suppose an advanced type of NAACP. And yet, he's out of touch. I thought if Browning had come to the man-in-the-street, black or white, and had said to him "Here is my plan, what do you think?" the guy probably would've said that it's not going to work. I think, perhaps, one reason Browning felt his plan would work was because he was wrapped up in his own world which was not only the world of books but a world in which he was the middle-classer going around collecting money for his organization.

WILLIAMS: But there are two things. First Browning's plan did

133

work. All he wanted to do was have the cop killed. He's not really responsible for the other things that happened. Second, the older we grow, the more cautious we tend to become about many things. He was very concerned about having this act done, but not being punished for initiating it himself—which also worked. When the other things started breaking up these were not at all related to Browning except that his original act sort of sparked everything else that happened.

Now, one of the reasons why, I suppose, I did that Browning thing was to somehow tell people that it doesn't matter how much education you've got if you're black. There's no such thing as removing one's self from it. You're always to some degree involved. And as Sartre, a Johnny-come-lately, has just said recently, the intellectual has got to put his body on the line as well as his mind. Now he says that knowing full well that many people are not about to do so. But, if you're talking about young intellectuals who are probably not that well known in France, that's a different story. They can be hurt. They can be killed. So, the question of putting one's body on the line with one's mind becomes something you might want to equivocate about. And that's exactly Browning's position.

CASH: You have the Don in *Sons of Darkness, Sons of Light* tell Browning that the mistake many people make is that they feel that being an intellectual, or being educated, and indulging in violence are mutually exclusive. I see reflected in the story with Browning and with some of the other characters the questions about the black student as a whole; that is, the student who would get a college education or more. His problem, a problem he's got to resolve, is how he's going to relate to his people, be they uneducated or educated, and get out of just sitting in on meetings with his peers.

WILLIAMS: I think that's a real big problem. There has been a lot of cry about the validity of the education in the American system, and that black people should not become a part of it. My point is I believe in education; not merely in formal education. All you can get through formal education is some desire to go further than you already are. And to that extent I think it would be a beautiful thing for a lot of kids who have doubts about going. Another thing, I've spoken to a number of these black kids on the campuses in their dashikies and Afros, who are on the arm, so to speak, in Upward Bound programs and equal education. They have gun drills in the basements of their homes and all the rest. They sort of over-react to finding themselves on this great highway to becoming middle class. But I call them middle class because one of the first routes to becoming middle class is to go to college. They called me an old Uncle Tom and so on. I can't help that. So we have a real problem with these kids—and there are more and more black kids going to colleges right now than ever before in American history—as to whether they're going to take this information and education that they're going to be exposed to and return to the people and apply it in some meaningful way or just be one of these guys who walks out of school and gets a job as vice president of I.B.M. I think there're a lot of kids who aren't really thinking of this. They're saying one thing, but very readily accepting something else. That's the problem.

CASH: You have Browning wonder, at one point in *Sons of Darkness, Sons of Light,* why black groups had to go the African route. Do you question this also?

WILLIAMS: I just feel that the African route is very deceptive. While I understand and approve of the new reaching back for roots, I think it only really works when there is a reciprocal action going on. Now the Africans by and large do not know and couldn't care less about what's going on in America. The elite give lots of lip service to our Brothers in America. They could have made it possible for black Americans with engineering, medical, teaching, social work skills to pass back and forth using their skills in Africa becoming really acquainted with the groups. But, they don't want that. I know because I've been there twice and I know people who have been social workers and scientists. I knew a guy who worked for the space station in Kano, Nigeria, who quit the U.S. government to go help the Nigerians. And they wouldn't have him. Last thing I heard he was selling chickens in a supermarket. So I think to be aware of Africa, I mean this in one basic sense, we've got to realize that we've been living all this time under the shame of having been slaves or having been brought from Africa; as the books tell us not really fighting too well to stay in Africa. My parents, their parents before them have all been trying to deal with this. And now we are dealing with it. It may be we're through dealing with the Afros and dashikies, and can deal realistically with Africa. I think we've got to say yes this is our homeland, this is where we came from, this is how we came. Now we're here and we're doing our thing. Maybe I'd like to go back over and take a tour. I would recommend it to every black American to go to Africa, if possible, and look around. But it's all been so damn superficial for me because I'm sick and tired of hearing about the ancient African empires in Kush and so on, because many more meaningful things took place there a long time ago. Our black scholars seem to stop at the 18th dynasty and so forth; instead of getting into, as the white archaeologists are, that diffusion of people all over the world, to the new world thousands of years before Columbus. There are all kinds of evidence that there were black people among them. We don't have any scholars, African or black American, that I know of who are getting into this thing, which in many ways is a hell of a lot more meaningful than dealing with Kush. This is why I feel a lot of it is superficial.

CASH: Maybe one reason the black Americans change their names and outfits is that it gives them a certain solidarity and emphasizes a heritage that they feel they do have. For many, too, I think, it's become a symbol of something more valiant, an external show of their defiance. Oh, I thought it significant that in *The Man Who Cried I Am,* you have the story of the King Alfred plan coming via an African.

WILLIAMS: Well, that was as good a place as any for it. By the way, I wear dashikies, too, occasionally. They're very comfortable.

CASH: To move to another facet of the novels, in *The Man Who Cried I Am* you have a betrayal. You have a betrayal in *Night Song* which is across racial lines. But, you have the slick Blacks in *The Man Who Cried I Am* who turned against Max and Harry. You have a similar thing happening in *Sons of Darkness*: Greene simply did not trust his friend, Trotman. What have you to say about all this lack of trust?

WILLIAMS: I think that's a basically human reason for falling out. When I was getting married for the second time and somebody asked me if I had known the girl long, I said quite long. And, he said the most valuable thing in the world is to be with someone that you can really trust. I thought about that a long time and I think he's actually right. I've been involved in many things with the Brothers and without the Brothers. There have always been areas of betrayal, kind of more vicious with the Brothers than with other people. Just incredibly vicious. I don't know what it is except that as far as I can see it's one of those human frailties that Shakespeare dealt with all the time. It's like when I was growing up in Syracuse and I felt some racial slight, I'd get salty and the teachers would say you got a chip on your shoulder, which means I either had been betrayed or wary that I was about to be betrayed or something.

CASH: Another statement made by Browning is that he will return to teaching, but he will teach down the system. That is his new resolve as the novel concludes. What do you feel about this?

WILLIAMS: I think this is pretty much what I am trying to do. When I go around lecturing, somebody might ask me about improvements in the country. I tell them about Albuquerque, for example, and ask why in the hell must I wait fifteen years so I can sleep in the Holiday Inn of all places. And this is what I like to think I am doing. I'm very pleased that I have three sons, which is not to belittle women, but I think that males tend to be prime movers. So, they're sort of like three new cables; I try to teach them, without being obvious about it, what's going down, what they should expect from themselves and so on. That's really what I mean.

CASH: About this idea of stereotype, many black writers rebelled against the white stereotype of Blacks by building an opposite stereotype. And so you get in some books and movies Blacks who would be super…

WILLIAMS: Super spade?

CASH: Yes. So, in trying to avoid one stereotype, one falls into another. Isn't the black author, like the black man in America, on the dodge from falling into stereotypes?

WILLIAMS: Actually I don't think there's been much reaction on the part of black writers to the white stereotype of black people. Sam Greenlee, of course, has a super spade in his book. I don't know that John Killens has ever dealt with a super spade, or Chester Himes, and I don't think that I did. I know I would like to. Maybe the guy who comes closest to it is Ishmael Reed. But, his characters are so satirical until you don't think of them as being super spades. That's an interesting point. I don't think there's been that much reaction as you say, except maybe in comic books. My oldest son does a lot of work with comic books in terms of teaching his kids. He has been collecting all these books that now have super Charlie and super Spade and they're fighting the crooks together. That's the area where you find it.

CASH: Well, maybe if you went to the area of the movies, you'd find this more prevalent.

WILLIAMS: I think it more viable in movies at this point than in novels. *Sons of Darkness, Sons of Light* in many ways was a pot boiler for me anyhow. I sat down and wrote it comparatively quickly compared to the other books. This was a reaction to my continued poverty after *The Man Who Cried I Am* came along. It looked as if finally, I'd be able to make a little money and help both the boys who were in college at that time. The critical acclaim was good, but I was just as poor as I had always been. And as a matter of fact, that book in paperback is all over the place, but the paperback publisher tells me it hasn't made a dime. The whole thing is so damn crazy it's better not to go into it. So, I sat down and wrote this book. I think it's one of my worse novels. It brought in more paperback money than *The Man Who Cried I Am*. And it's just the way things happen in America. The things that are crap or tend to be crap, or are not as good as other things, always for some reason do better.

CASH: Do you have a pessimistic outlook for militant organizations mobilizing?

WILLIAMS: Yes, I do. In the first place—it may be a black thing, I don't know—we seem to abhor secrecy. You can't have a militant black group in this country unless it's infiltrated. It's just impossible. The only groups you can have that're valid and functioning and haven't done anything yet are those that operate in total secrecy. We just don't seem to be able to pull that off. I think that's what's totally necessary in this society that is shot through with surveillance systems, peoples, codes, and so forth.

CASH: In your novels you've shown us characters who try one way which mightn't be as effective as they might want so they will go another way. As you say in the last line of *Sons of Darkness,* this is the way with things, the rhythms of trial and error, of going from one plan to another. What would you then propose for Blacks struggling for equality? What idea might you have that would be more workable?

WILLIAMS: I don't know if it would be more workable, but I guess one gets a little desperate. As I said before, it's kind of a far out plan. But, it is that of employing, utilizing black people who look like whites. The number, I think, is about twenty or thirty million, which is pretty close to the whole population of Spain or Great Britain. That's a lot of people. Utilizing some of these people to infiltrate into the technological systems of the armed forces over a period of years, several years, maybe half a century or so. And at some point just everyone in concert pushing a button that dismantles the whole goddamn thing. And there you have it, a

138

technological collapse, which means an economic collapse. And in terms of relationships with other world powers, they would no longer exist.

CASH: In *The Man Who Cried I Am,* you have Max and Harry running into some static because they had flirted with communism. What are your feelings particularly about the Marxist doctrine as it tried to encompass Blacks?

WILLIAMS: I think it's pretty obviously failed; mainly because black people were never its initial thrust. When Marx, Lenin, Trotsky and others spoke about exploited people, they were thinking mostly of the exploited peoples of Europe. It really wasn't until the end of the second World War that the communists started to leave the Asian-European mainland and go to Africa or the Caribbean. And again that's an example, particularly with the Asians, of what I was saying with the plan in this new novel [*Captain Blackman*]. Guys like Chou En-lai and Mao and the big man [Ho Chi Minh] who died in Hanoi recently—all those guys were involved in Marxism at a very early period and really only came to be powerful people, let's say, in the late '30's, shortly before World War II. They got their own following during World War II. That's a long time. And it's that kind of patience that I think is going to be required of any change in this system, if the damn thing holds together long enough. But as you said about going back to the Bahamas [the interviewer's birthplace], after this prolonged study there may be nothing to go back to. That's always a big problem.

The basic thrust of the Marxist is history. And black American history was something they, just like black Americans themselves, knew very little of, and what they knew they did not bother to utilize. For example, they did a lot of work in the South, or they thought they were going to do a lot of work in the South, but they didn't reckon on the kinds of opposition they were going to have from the crackers. Just tremendous opposition. Then they started in the urban centers: New York, Chicago, San Francisco, Los Angeles. But as Chester Himes points out even among the communists, say, who were highly placed in the arts, the black communist was still a black man. He'd have to eat in the kitchen if he came to pick up something from those people.

CASH: In *The Man Who Cried I Am* as Max attempts to elude his assassins, he says to himself that he had really come to realize that America had pushed Blacks to a choice. It was either going to be

139

destruction or otherwise peaceful co-existence. In *Sons of Darkness, Sons of Light,* the same thought is echoed. One character says that it was silly to try to revamp a system that had insanity at its very core. These are dark, gloomy pronouncements. Yet, I can't help but note that the novels still end with some hope. Is that an ambivalence that you share personally?

WILLIAMS: I don't think it's a personal ambivalence. I think it's a human ambivalence. You want things to go on. You have to have hope for two reasons: first, if not you have to jump off a bridge like Hart Crane or somebody and I don't think I'm anywhere near doing that. Number two is that as long as you have the hope, there are things that you can do to bring about those things that you hope will happen for the better, either physically or by writing or what have you. I think this is the only thing that's made it work as awkwardly as it has—there have been a lot of people who have hoped that Armageddon wouldn't come. Maybe just by virtue of saying hello to a nigger with a smile one morning, that sort of puts it off for another day. So you operate on that premise.

CASH: Well, let's leave this topic for a while and go to another area in which the Black has been slighted by the media and sociological study: that of the black woman and mother, her role in the family throughout the years and how, perhaps, this led you to write *Sissie.*

WILLIAMS: You mentioned earlier that in reaction to the white stereotype of the happy-go-lucky darkie that there might come about a super spade. I think this kind of reaction has really happened in terms of black mothers. Not in novels so much, but maybe articles. I read something not too long ago, one of a continuing number of pieces, which deals with the great, good and golden strength of black mothers in raising their children. I think that's a reaction, because the fact of the matter is that black mothers are no worse or no better than any other kind of mother. But we get into this thing because somebody said black mothers are no damned good and what we do is create a black Mary Magdalene. As for black women in general, the same thing is going on. A friend of mine did a piece last summer in *The New York Times* on why black women are not interested in women's lib. And she said a lot of foolish things to be a very intelligent woman which was that black women had more sensuality and a basic sex thing than white women. And that black men really ain't shit and are totally in awe of the system. I had lunch with her and asked why she wrote all that bullshit. She couldn't really backtrack, but she was hemming and hawing for about twenty minutes giving me her explanations. I think she realized that it was kind of silly—particularly since publications like *The New York Times* and many others in this country will only publish pieces by black writers if they say pretty much what the editors of those publications think or want them to say. For her to have done a piece regaling the sensuality of black women and the worthlessness of black men is like playing right into their hands. It's one of the things I think black writers have to be aware of these days. Other writers have not had to be bothered with those kinds of political overtones in their work.

CASH: It seems to me a real irony that Sissie says at one point she never had a dream of her own because she just wanted her children to be able to dream. Yet, this is not sufficient to convince her daughter Iris to love her. And even the son would not bring his family to his mother's death because he didn't want them to be contaminated in any way. The way the novel works appeals to me most. I don't think it can really be compared, because it's a whole different type of novel, to *The Man Who Cried I Am,* for instance.

WILLIAMS: The structures are the only things that are similar. I like *Sissie.* As a matter of fact, Ralph Joplin is coming back in one of these new novels I'm working on. He's one of these guys who comes for this reunion. You know, I think there has been, ironically, at least for people in my generation, this great emphasis on education. Your children have got to do better than we did. That's human nature. That's how evolution expands and expounds. But I see that it's a very costly process with great numbers of people I know. In the circle in which I grew up three of the guys turned out to be homosexuals. Lots of pressures. Lots of very strange things going on. And now all for what? I still maintain that education is to be valued as a starting point. Now my parents, for example, can sit back and say they did all this for what. I've got the same problems of racism that they had, maybe more subtle, maybe not so immediate, maybe not so harsh, but the end result is all the same. So, I find now that both my parents, who have always been acutely aware of racism and disgusted, made us aware of it—they went through a period when things weren't so bad; but right now you talk about those "militant" kids, I don't think there's anybody more militant than people

141

my parents' age. They're in their late sixties and time is running out. They can look back over their lifetimes and the lifetimes of their children and parts of the lifetimes of their parents and see that only inches have been gained. They've got to be salty.

The whole business with black families, again, is a reaction to so much of the white sociological documentation on how poorly off the black family was or is without understanding that however a family is composed, it has to function. It must function or go under. Very often it doesn't matter whether there are two parents there or one parent or no parent. Things have to go on. There's been enough experimentation and documentation in other societies—the Israeli society, for example, where they proved it's not necessary to have parents around. They raise the kids in kibbutz nursery. What the hell is a parent? It's just a vehicle and a lot of us, like myself, of course, are on great ego trips when we think we're that important to our children. I imagine to a certain extent we are, but physiologically it's also been established that when parents, say, of monkeys aren't around or even of people, baby monkeys or baby children will find something else to love.

CASH: I was thinking back to the problem of education and this idea of pushing which you do deal with in *Sissie*. It seems very realistic that the child who is pushed to the extent of feeling that he's not loved but simply being used as an instrument for parents' aims—that child will grow up with some remorse and antipathy toward the very field that he's become adept in and to the parents who pushed him into it. There is also a possibility of such a reaction on the part of the child even when the parents mean well. Doesn't this make getting one's children educated a risky business?

WILLIAMS: I think as long as education is still socially accepted by the majority, there'll be no problem with kids wanting to be educated. I never even really had to discuss it with my two older boys. They were just determined that they were going to college. Determined is even the wrong word. They just felt it was their goddamn duty to go to college; maybe simply because I had gone. One even went to my school which he didn't necessarily have to do. The other one didn't. I tried to dissuade my oldest boy from taking divinity studies, but I did that rather subtly, I think. As a result, he found his own direction. That's really been the extent of my involvement in their educational processes. I've tried to dissuade my other son from becoming a writer because he can write at any time. I thought he would have more value to the revolution by becoming a constitutional lawyer, for example. He said he would think about it.

CASH: What about education and Blacks? After all, if education is the way of introducing you to the system, when you do become educated, if it has been "successful," doesn't it make you then much more apathetic, systematized, or more prone to accept things without complaint? Isn't education, then, a way of quelling militancy?

WILLIAMS: Well, it's always seemed to me that I was like a spy in the educational system going in to see how Charlie works. Then I could bring this back and tell my sons, friends and relatives what's really going down. I think it's more important to become involved in this kind of educational system than a lot of people realize. Simply because you cannot stand outside and think about conducting any kind of a revolution if you don't know what the enemy is doing. It's sort of like a patrol. You have to know what the other guy is doing so you send your patrol out always to keep in contact with them, so that you know when he's going to launch an attack over this bridge or over this plain. Unless you're in contact with him, you won't know.

I keep running into lots of black kids who claim that they will not read white writers. That is suicide. Again for the same reasons. In order to know how the system works you have to study it, know it. Otherwise how can you get out here and talk about revolution? Against what? Just because the guy is white (which obviously is very often reason enough)? But you have to know how he's working within that whiteness in order to successfully subvert what he's doing or overcome it or whatever. So I really have no patience for people who say they don't want to get involved in that system. Because when they say they don't want to get involved in that system, what they're really saying is "If I do baby, I'm long gone, because Charlie's got me" instead of going in there and getting what's to be derived and coming out and bringing it back to the people. That is my view of participating in the educational system.

CASH: Another idea that comes to mind is that starting with *The Angry Ones,* you portray Steve Hill's boss as a homosexual. You have a homosexual patron in *The Man Who Cried I Am* where you also have numerous scenes of the cobalt treatment for Max's cancer of the anus. I saw all this as saying that if Blacks are to get anywhere they've got to

143

kiss asses or surrender their masculinity, their very backbones. If Steve had pandered to his boss's seduction efforts, he would have been on the way to getting a raise and more. Max could have had more popularity than he did, if he would have played up to Granville.

WILLIAMS: Let me begin that answer with a quote from Ishmael Reed. "In America," he says, but I think it's true everywhere, "art is cock." I think this is pretty true. I don't know about that cobalt machine. And I wasn't, not consciously, dealing with the kinds of things a black man would have to do in order to enter the system. But obviously as you point out with Rollie and Granville things could have been a lot different had Steve and Max pandered to them. I guess I was dealing from my experiences in this business in terms of how one can become a success or not. Very often the avenues to success are blocked by people who are homosexual, or at the most, bisexual. There's no gainsaying the fact that Jimmy Baldwin's tremendous success lay in great part in his being homosexual. No doubt whatsoever in the black literary community or the white literary community. I make this judgment on the basis of Hernton's article (Calvin Hernton, "Blood of the Lamb" in *Amistad 1,* ed. Williams and Charles Harris, New York: Random House, 1970). I've not been directly approached. Everybody knows I'm straight, so that's that. If people know that, then it's pretty well all right. But what they look for is some sign of weakness. For example, I was twelve years between marriages. And I don't know how they viewed me, but I had a great time. I mean I had twelve years of just fun from one end of the world to the next. But the single status may have triggered something in their own minds about how I was.

These two instances with Granville and Rollie—these two characters are drawn on characters who are very obvious and prevalent in the black and white literary community. They're very real obstacles. One of the reasons why LeRoi Jones is always talking about faggot white men is that he's gone through the same thing. I know so many black artists in Europe who are ostensibly straight people, but who basically are not. We have Black Power and Jewish Power and all those other Powers; there is also the presence of Gay Power and it is not one to be dismissed in the Arts and elsewhere.

CASH: In *Night Song,* Keel suffers impotency because of Della. This reinforces the idea of the Black being sort of castrated or his very potency being affected in relation to the White.

WILLIAMS: I think that's a little bit obtuse. As I recall, he became impotent because of rage. It was a question of hurting this woman through the sexual act, which he didn't want to do. So, he short-circuited himself and he became impotent. I guess the effect is really the same, though, isn't it?

CASH: Yes. I would like to get your comment on interracial marriage.

WILLIAMS: I get a lot of questions from young black female students and some time not so young and often not students. The vogue right now is that this black man-white woman thing has got to go. That's really becoming a terrible thing to handle in New York. Although the evidence is that no matter how much people complain about it, that's exactly what's happening. Interracial marriages are increasing. A lot of black women have basically idiotic reasons for being opposed to this. And sometimes the reasons are not so idiotic because here in 1971 any woman is open to competition, I don't care if she's got polka dots. Black women realize this, and they appear to be reluctant to enter into combat for black men. So, they will very often sit back and talk rather than act. It's, as far as I can determine, not a question of preference as much as happenstance, one of the things I dealt with in *The Man Who Cried I Am*. Cecil Brown, on the other hand, who wrote *Life and Loves of Mr. Jiveass Nigger*—his whole thesis is that white women treat black men better. But, it all gets down to individuals. They must make the decisions and nobody can make them for them.

Interracial couples appear in my novels because that's pretty much the life I've lived. I grew up in a community that was well mixed in Syracuse at that time. It was not a ghetto as black ghettos now go. We had all kinds of people. I played house with all kinds of girls. That was the way I grew up. My first wife was black. At the end of that marriage, girlfriends have just been about anything that was there and willing and we had a thing together. My second wife is white. We know a lot of mixed couples. I can't say any of them are having problems as a result of this new thing that's going around. I think it's something that will pass. It's again a part of the revolutionary rhetoric. How for example can a black man be less faithful to his race by virtue of having a white wife? And you would still praise Frederick Douglass, for example: we get out and do this for Fred Douglass; we get out and do that for whoever else was great and had a white wife. These are things we don't take into consideration. This is what makes me think it's a passing thing with the revolution; which is not to say that the gals aren't sincere when they're bitching. But, we've got to deal with some of these things not always on a purely emotional level, and it's not always a way out to say that we are an emotional people. Of course, we are. But we have to use something of the intellectual process to mitigate pure, destructive, if it's always going to be that way, emotionalism. I know what they're talking about, and I don't know what they expect me to do. Run and hide, or what? I have to go on doing my thing. As it's happened, some of the most vociferous people like Nikki Giovanni, who obviously with a name like that comes out of some kind of a white background, was death on this two or three years ago. But she's not now. So, I think things pass.

I've been to some places like the Caribbean, for example, where black people wouldn't look at me twice until my wife came up beside me; probably saying, "Oh, that cat's got a white wife. He must be something special." Then they'll start relating to me. The whole thing is really so screwed up and sick that I just can't be involved. I'm forty-six or forty-seven and I've got a lot of things to do. I just can't be bothered with all that silly bullshitting. As far as I'm concerned, that's really what it is. Suppose I took my wife out, shot her, and I said, "Okay, I'm free. Now one of you babes marry me." Maybe I'll get a lot of offers now 'cause I'm what they would consider a successful writer. But the times I went through with my first wife when I was sitting down there writing—Oh Lord!—and even after that with the girlfriends I had who were black and a number of white girlfriends: "You're a writer! How are we going to live?" And that just sort of took care of that. There you are on interracial marriages. That's my view.

CASH: One friend of mine disliked *The Man Who Cried I Am* mainly because of the mixture of realism; particularly your using characters who were such close parallels to actual people.

WILLIAMS: I really don't know what he was complaining about. It seems more and more fiction is written this way in any case, the *roman à clef*. I'd have to ask him if he raised the same objections to William Styron's *Nat Turner* which is quite baldly and incorrectly based

146

on a black hero. I find truth is more real than fiction. But you can't always present the truth as the truth. So you have no choice but to present it in fiction.

CASH: Yeah, Alain Robbe-Grillet makes that same point. You mentioned in your books some of the difficulties the black writer faces. Is it the black writer's duty to write black? That is, to write about his race and try to contribute some way through that writing?

WILLIAMS: I think the black writer has two functions of equal importance. One is that given this time and its processes, he really has to deal with and for his people. He has to become an educator, a teacher, a storyteller, a satirist, any vehicle that will help make his people aware of their positions. At the same time, he's also bound to become an expert in his craft: writing a novel, writing poetry, what have you. The most important thing is the message. I would like to feel that the better the craft, the smoother the message comes out. A clumsy vehicle delivers a clumsy message. A smooth vehicle delivers a clear message. That's what black writing should be about. Also, to the extent that the American novel form has thus far served us so poorly in terms of how we appear in them, as they're written by Whites, we really ought to try to experiment with the novel form. Turn it around. Find something else that we can do either to advance it so that it becomes a better vehicle for our message or to make it so that a novel written by Norman Mailer will be so outdated that he'll have to sit down and write like us.

CASH: Is there a distinguishing element about black fiction? I was once asked is there such a thing as black literature, as a genre. When one reads a novel say by Alan Paton, what's to make that distinguishable from, say, a novel by Richard Wright? Can one not get the same aesthetic appreciation from John Howard Griffin's experiment as from another by a black author?

WILLIAMS: Well, I think that's a little complicated to answer. There is a black literature simply because white critics have demanded that black literature exist. Not only the critics, the college systems have done this. An instructor will teach a course in the black novel while he really should be dealing with a course in the American novel with black authors. Hell, Chester Himes and Richard Wright were contemporaries of Hemingway. John O. Killens is a contemporary of Norman Mailer, so is Jimmy Baldwin, so am I. But the insistence is on teaching these writers in isolation. This may turn out to be a pretty big boomerang: a boomerang in the sense that if maybe you've got five or six black authors, or maybe you go back like Saunders Redding did and you get a whole spectrum, what happens is that the kids who know nothing about black writers say, "My God, I haven't even heard of some of these guys." Out of a course like that somebody might ask about other black writers. You name ten or twelve and after a while they're going to start believing some of the things that we say about censorship, and how difficult it is or was for black writers to get published. Then you have to really start to worry about why is this so. The student may think, "Last year I couldn't believe there was one single black writer in all of American history. This year I'm assigned to read an eight hundred page book that's filled with nothing but niggers. What's going on?" It's crazy.

To the extent that you're dealing with Alan Paton's writings or John Howard Griffin's—and as much as I despise the man, I suppose some people would want to put William Faulkner in the same group—the presence of works like theirs sort of makes it truthful what we used to say years ago before we were deeply involved in the revolution and dealing really only with black people; that is, we're dealing with a universality. And it may be black but it's still universal. When a guy like Paton sets out to write or Griffin or Bernard Malamud in his new book in which the black character is very badly done, aren't those guys saying once they attack a subject like that that there must be some humanity in it, some validity in it which makes what we've been saying all along to be quite truthful? So, if black literature exists, there's going to be a boomerang, and it's more than black literature.

CASH: Do you think we'll also have a backlash in or against Black Studies?

WILLIAMS: There is today a gathering effort on the part of some of the establishment to curtail, contain, and perhaps eliminate Black Studies. That's the backlash, but I do believe that Black Studies will improve and last, perhaps, in better forms than those now in existence. Then, there are rumors now in New York that black writing is finished. I don't know. It's probably true since more writing is handled in New York as a commodity in any case. It may be true that people have had it with this package. I know that book salesmen say one thing in New York, but when they're out on the road, they do something else all together. I've always felt that the time would come when the doors would swing closed on this great surge of black literature. I still think it might, but I don't think it's going to close as tightly as it did against the so-called Harlem Renaissance. There're many more people involved now. There are more white editors who are trying to perceive this literature as being more than just a commodity. There are a few black editors, none of whom are really top notch, but maybe they'll get there. The presence of some black editors offers a little bit of insurance; not much, but more so than ten years ago. Some of it will be cut back. Quite frankly, if I can speak as a man who has some degree of pride in his craft or skill, I think some of it should be cut back. Because they're so busy hustling black writers as a commodity, they're really publishing a lot of shit. Black people are not fools, you know. They say, well Jesus Christ, the time is here now. I'm going to write me forty-five poems and the first one will be called "White Cunt." I've seen poems like this. The next will be called "Off the Pig." And the third one will be called "Charlie I'm Going to Kick Your Ass." They send them in and they're published. It's really laughable but in the long run detrimental not only to the masses of black people, who are just as conservative as the masses of white people and don't want to read that stuff—it's detrimental to the black writer who's done this because he thinks he's produced a work of art, a skillful work, when in reality he's done no such thing. He's invested very little time or energy in studying his craft. When I say studying his craft, the only way you can study writing is to read, read, read. A lot of these kids don't want to read, and they wind up short all the time.

CASH: Commercialism. I wonder about this, and I'll just muse a while then you can give me your comments. Your paperback novels have a black man and white woman on the cover as if that's going to be the crux of the novel. But it's a commercial technique. I wonder what this commercialism does to the whole movement of black interests. Then, too, I was watching television the other day and saw some Chicanos wearing large sombreros and decked out in the Mexican garb. It was quite commercialized. There are people who sell these things and make profit out of this desire to maintain one's heritage. What do you make of all this?

WILLIAMS: One of the things I noticed with some sadness while walking around Albuquerque this morning was that everybody's making

149

money off the Indians and the old Spanish thing except the Indians and Mexicans.

Let's start first with the soft cover jackets. You don't have any control over that. You hope that they will be tasteful. They never are. I wrote to Pocket Books when they brought out three books with a black guy and white woman on the cover. I wrote to the editor. I said this is really bullshitty, because I think what you're doing is turning off buyers. This is what went in 1950. It's not going now. I never heard from them. It shows the kind of racist nature that editors are still involved with. This is what's going to sell books. We'll put this darkie up here with this blond. I don't think that a hell of a lot of black people are buying books with jackets like that anymore. What this also means is that they don't give a damn about black readers, too. That kind of commercialism would be bad if it were only a question of money. As I say it's racism as well, which is worse. I bought an Afro pick. I thought it was wood. It was made of plastic. Macy's now sells dashikis. And I'll bet you ten to one, the biggest company putting out Afro wigs is white. But what do you do? You stop wearing dashikis? You stop wearing wigs, or you stop wearing Afros? Then who's going to manufacture the combs?

CASH: Or the shirts?

WILLIAMS: If there's one thing black people need to understand about this man, and most black people don't, it's that anything that comes down the pike is saleable. If you're involved with a man who will sell other people, you know goddamn well he'll sell anything. Maybe black people know this in some small distant part of their souls, but they sure act like they never heard of it before.

I came out here for an inclusive fee of six hundred bucks. I thought there would be a real black group here. Well, I find that it's very small, but I'll get a chance to see whoever is in it tomorrow. By the time I get through with all this, I'll probably clear about one hundred fifty dollars. But we've got guys who won't leave Newark or Chicago for less than $700, $800, or $1,000 clear to talk about the black revolution to a lot of white folks. We were talking earlier about being so depressed with the things that are going on. Those guys are just as repetitious and greedy as the man is. So it makes very little point for them to stand up and talk about how bad this man is when they are probably worse than he is or at least just as bad.

CASH: I would like to know something about your early life.

WILLIAMS: I was the oldest of four living children. I've got a brother and two sisters. I went to public schools in Syracuse: Washington Irving grade school, Madison Junior High. I went to both Central High School, where I played football, basketball, ran track, and 'Vocational High School. I didn't graduate from high school before going into the service. I was in the Navy for three years and I came out and I finished.

CASH: What year was it that you went in?

WILLIAMS: That was 1943. I came out of the Navy in '46, January, I think. I was in for just about three years. Finished high school that year and went to college that year. It was a very curious thing. I got married that year, too. I did a lot of things that year. Years later I had a discussion with my ex-wife about, I don't know how it came up, but I wanted to tell the boys that I hadn't finished high school before I was twenty-one or close to twenty-one. But for some reason, she was pretty shocked at this. I said what's wrong with that? I don't know if she had implanted some kind of groovy image about how smooth things were. So anyhow I told them. They said okay, fine. I wanted them to know so they wouldn't have any misconceptions about the kind of life I had as a young man, as a teenager. It was rough sometimes and sometimes it wasn't. I went to work sometimes, I went to school sometimes. Had a lot of friends, many of whom I still have.

Anyhow my wife and I were married. I was going to school and raising a family. Greg was born in the next year, '47 or '48. I was going to school, working part time and we were living mainly on the GI bill and my part-time work which carried me into the foundries sometimes. Worked as a hospital orderly. A lot of jobs. Things you do to keep body and soul together. We broke up in '53 or '54 and divorced a couple of years later. I lived in California for a while. I worked for a black insurance company, which was an experience. I came back to New York City so I could be close to the kids; got a job in a Vanity Publishing House. This was the setting for *The Angry Ones*. I worked there for about a year and was writing *The Angry Ones* at that time. I asked for a raise the next year and the man said you're fired.

I published a weekly newspaper, an 8½ x 11 newsletter called the *Negro Market Newsletter*. I'd also done some publicity and public relations in Syracuse on a part-time basis and in California for NBC and

151

CBS. So I thought I was knowledgeable enough to start a paper that would be for white advertising and public relations agencies dealing with the Negro market, which everybody was talking about at that time. I would gather the news, write it, lay it out, take it to the printer, pick it up, fold it and mail it every week. My big allies at that time were the black guys who were Negro market specialists within those agencies. I thought this, but as it happened, they turned out to be the very people who killed it because they thought it was too good. After all, they were doing what I was doing. If this newspaper kept going around, they wouldn't have any jobs. So they didn't take the subscriptions they promised to and a few other things like that. Then I was really on my ass for a while because this thing really hadn't made any money and I was living on unemployment which at that time was $36 a week; my room rent was $20. I made out, I mean I lived, I survived. There were times I got odd jobs that brought in a little money. I stayed with friends on two occasions. I just sort of fell into things: an advertising agency job, an assistant to a book publisher who was a psychopath, then I went to work for the American Committee on Africa. By that time I had managed to save a little money so I went to Spain for a while. Came back and was involved in doing a lot of radio work for a station in New York. The year I came home from Europe *The Angry Ones* was published. Then I did *Night Song* and *Sissie*. I worked on those together. *Night Song* was finished first and I got the contract with Farrar, Straus, and Giroux plus I'd done another book that came out when *Sissie* came out in '63, a book on Africa for children. So, I had a little money. It wasn't a lot, but people would call on me to do reviews. I was also limping along doing magazine articles. Then in 1963 *Holiday Magazine* asked me to do what John Steinbeck had done in his book *Travels with Charley,* which resulted from his driving around the country. He did that in '60, I think. Now they wanted a black man to do it and I did. *Holiday* was the best magazine in the country at that time. It was like a real shot for whatever career I thought I was into. I did that and it was a pretty big success. That's really been the difference. And like they say, here I am.

CASH: Between '63 and '67 did you do further European travelling?

WILLIAMS: Yes. I went on a very long jaunt in early '64 right after I finished the *Holiday* piece. I worked on the second draft while I was travelling through Europe, Israel, and Africa. As a matter of fact, I sent the second draft back from Addis Ababa. I guess I was away for six or seven months that time, most of it in Africa. I got back to the U.S. in '64 and went back to Africa in '65 to do a television show. Later in '65 I married again. We spent a year in Europe mostly in Spain and Amsterdam. I think I've been back three times since then.

CASH: Seems that the experiences of Max and Harry in *The Man Who Cried I Am* parallel your own.

WILLIAMS: Actually I could see the times when Max was like myself. Because I had done some work for *Newsweek* in Africa with a specific job in mind to look for a desk in West Africa. I had been down to the Congo and a few other places. I had covered part of the Ethiopian-Somali war for *Newsweek*. But in the main, Chester Himes was my Max. His was the figure I held up pretty much.

CASH: Many critiques of *The Man Who Cried I Am* focus on the King Alfred plan. I think a fascination with that conclusion alone really cheats the rest of the novel and its art.

WILLIAMS: I agree with you completely. Whenever I go someplace, that's the only thing people ask me about. It's getting awful.

CASH: I have run out of questions. Is there anything else you'd like to mention?

WILLIAMS: I want you to read these last two chapters of this new novel [*Captain Blackman*]. This is structured kind of strange and it uses a lot of documentary material. Before each section there is a quote which is for real or a documentary sentence. It tells you what the next part is going to be about. This section is about the murder of two hundred black soldiers during World War II by the American army.

I seem to be publishing a number of books with angry in the title. Today I wouldn't have to take that kind of crap from publishers. *My* title for *The Angry Ones* was *One for New York*. As you know, this was published as a soft cover original. If it hadn't been published at that time I probably would have tried to forget about writing all together. It had been written five years earlier, and I was really close to hanging up the whole business. So when they said they wanted to make the title something that's going to grab people, I was powerless to stop it. I did a paperback anthology that was called *The Angry Black*. Now again this was after I published *Night Song* and *Sissie*. In this field, power is relative, you see. Even at that point I didn't have the power to say no, you aren't going to use that because I'm not dealing with anger here, I'm dealing with something else. But the publisher felt he could sell books if he had anger in the title. So that particular edition went into a hard cover edition with another publisher who felt that there should be some consistency between editions. Then New American Library republished an edition in soft cover of the same damn book with very few additions and angry was in the title again. I never believe in tipping my hand that way. That's one thing if you're black you learn. If you're angry, control it until you're in a situation where you can really do something about it.

We were talking about black musicians and about Eagle before. Eagle, as you may not know, is really based on Charlie Parker who was one of the most electric images in modern jazz. I had previously published an article on Charlie Parker and had planned to do a nonfictional book on him. I had a lot of information at my disposal. Eagle was, as I say, based on the Charlie Parker figure.

Returning to *Captain Blackman* I wanted originally to do it as a nonfictional book, but I kept running into stone walls. I couldn't raise the magazine money to travel to the places where I wanted to go to get the material. I'm talking about contemporary material. The historical material I had. Wherever I went, I did go to two or three army bases in America, I had those captains and lieutenants hanging on my shoulders. Magazines were not interested in a black man's view of black people in the army. They only wanted the story told by a white guy. A few years ago everybody was talking about this new democracy in the army. This was a white man's interpretation of what was going on. It turns out to have been false. If I had been able to raise the money to do those pieces, the first places I would have gone to would have been the stockades. That's where the truth always is—in the jails. Maybe my reputation preceded me. Not only was I not able to raise the money, but I had difficulty in getting clearance from the Pentagon to make the trip to Viet Nam, Thailand, and places like that. So, I decided to do it as a novel just to show that what I wanted to say, I wanted to say badly enough to do it in one form or another.

Interview—June 9, 1972

(In mid-May, 1972, John A. Williams and I met in New York. On my way to Syracuse University to study his manuscripts, I stopped off in

New York City for an informal chat and a copy of *Captain Blackman*, then just released. Almost a month later I returned to the City and on Friday, June 9, 1972, Mr. Williams, his son, Dennis, Mrs. Gloria Dickinson—a New Jersey teacher interested in the author's political thoughts—and myself spent most of the day discussing Williams' writings. My questions centered on *Captain Blackman* since it was the most recent work.)

CASH: *Captain Blackman* brought to mind Arna Bontemps' *Black Thunder* (1936), an account of Gabriel's revolt in 1880. I wonder if you were inspired by that work?

WILLIAMS: No, I don't think so. I read it about three years before, at the time of the Styron controversy [a reference to several black critics' reaction to William Styron's *The Confessions of Nat Turner*] and I was struck by what happened when a white man did an account of a slave revolt and the attendant publicity and what happened when Bontemps' book was reissued. It was reissued to almost a complete silence. It didn't influence me in any way.

CASH: Another comment relating to *Black Thunder*, you wrote in John Henrik Clarke's *William Styron's Nat Turner*, and I quote, "If, however, *Black Thunder* were to be published tomorrow, it would not have the slightest chance of making critics and readers reconsider their thoughts on history as it involved slaves." What, then, do you expect *Captain Blackman* will do as it involved black history?

WILLIAMS: I don't know what it's going to do. I know what I wanted it to do and that was again to give black readers some of the history they haven't had. The reaction of my publisher to that book was very strange. A lot of the white editors, male white editors, really liked it. But almost to a man, and I've heard this outside that particular circle, almost to a man what they talk about is that touching—I'm quoting now——touching scene between Abraham and the Indian. They don't talk about the slaughter of black troops in Italy or anything else. And as I haven't read any reviews, I don't know what the reviewers are saying or what sections they're dealing with. But it's like they really don't want to deal with the basic premise of the book, which I hope will come through with the young black readers.

CASH: I suppose the point I was trying to make is if you felt that should *Black Thunder* be re-released today it might have very little chance of affecting the readers' views on the position of slaves in history, why should you be more optimitic with your book and its affecting the black soldiers' place in history

WILLIAMS: But, there's a difference. There's a confluence of events, here. One is that as long as Bontemps has been around, he hasn't gained, which ever way you want to look at it, the notoriety or the publicity that I've got. So that I think there'd be a greater tendency on the part of younger people to read a book that I had done than to read something that Bontemps had done. I don't mean to belittle Bontemps at all. He's a prolific writer who possesses an amazing depth that some young black writers will never be able to match. He deserves far, far more than he's received at the hands of readers and critics alike. And if he's bitter about his treatment or lack of it, he certainly doesn't show it. Probably more due to my book on King than to *The Man Who Cried I Am*, I think a few more people read me, for perhaps the wrong reasons, I don't know. Furthermore, although still small given the population ratio, the black reading public is infintely larger today than it was in 1936 or 37 when *Black Thunder* was originally published. When it was re-released at the time Styron's book came out, one could feel that it was to shoot Styron down or at least make critics draw comparisons. But the critics having done their hoopdedoos over Nat Turner as drawn by Styron, weren't about to take back what they said. In other words, they bent over backwards to ignore it—*Black Thunder*—and did it very well. I had no such experience.

CASH: In returning to Henrik Clarke's book of criticism on *Nat Turner,* in your essay there you criticize Styron for not being "both a novelist and a historian." Did you set out to show him how it should be done?

WILLIAMS: No, I didn't set out to teach anybody lessons. I'd set something for myself, and that is—I don't know if we've talked about this—but I don't like to write the same book over and over again. For me writing novels is sort of like playing jazz, you improvise, you try to do new things, extend yourself more than you have with the previous book. That's all I was trying to do. If he happens to learn anything from it, so much the better.

CASH: But you would say you've capitalized on the mistakes you thought Styron made?

WILLIAMS: I don't know. I think his basic fault was to take what was historically accurate and ignore it. And all I've done is to take what is historically accurate and put it on a fictional basis. I happen to think that if you're going to write historical fiction, that's the only way to do it.

CASH: Well, going specifically to *Captain Blackman*, you have characters in there with special or particular names like Abraham and Gideon and Little David, all Biblical names from the Old Testament. Did you have some significance behind that selection?

WILLIAMS: The Abraham and Ishmael thing is self-explanatory. Little David in one of the earlier drafts was to be a regimental bugler. I think in the later drafts, I just forgot that. But, I think also, I was working sort of subconsciously along the lines of what would have been a guy's name given that time and place in history.

CASH: That brings me to Mimosa. What about that name?

WILLIAMS: In an earlier draft there was an explanatory note. Mimosa is a flower that when you touch it, it closes up.

CASH: A touch-me-not.

WILLIAMS: Right. And in a later draft that just got lost. But I wanted some essence of that for people who know flowers to sort of carry on.

CASH: That's the association I made.

WILLIAMS: Well, you know flowers. I'm sure a lot of people might wonder. But then I do things with that name in different times, like Osa and Mims. As you also noticed, perhaps, a lot of the names carry throughout history. The same guys who serve in the Viet Nam company serve in other companies and so on.

CASH: Mimosa is illiterate, a slave, and she is raped by white soldiers the first time she appears. The second time she is a student at Drake. And the last time she is in the foreign service in Saigon and has lots of power and influence. So, from the first time you meet Mimosa to the last, she progresses both career-wise and, of course, in physique. She's described in the beginning as being small, but the last time you see her the word you use is "Amazonian." And one soldier reflects that Mimosa and Blackman go together as they're both big in stature. What did you intend the reader to make of this progression of Mimosa through time, through history? Was this some commentary, maybe, on the black woman?

WILLIAMS: Yes, that was pretty subconscious. All I was trying to do was fit her as a viable black woman into each situation in which she appears: the World War I thing, the World War II thing and the Viet Nam thing. And I don't think any more than that, but when you were asking the question I said to myself, wow, maybe on the subconscious level, I was doing all those things.

CASH: Woodcock, a medic, is called Newblack because of his light skin. One character notes that he would not be recognizable as black if it weren't for his Afro.

WILLIAMS: I don't think I meant that simply to mean because he was fair. Mostly it's been my observation that the most militant black folks—and maybe this is a contradiction in terms of what I have to say—most militant black folks tend to be fair and I find that they have the biggest Afros and so on. But I think I must have been thinking of that with Woodcock. And also by Newblack I meant not only the physical arrangement of things but people who seem to have just recently become conscious of the fact that they're black.

CASH: Woodcock is the same person who in the end pulls off the coup. As Alain Locke pronounced the New Negro in the twenties, are you pronouncing the lighter-skinned Blacks like Woodcock as New Blacks, a possible strategic weapon in the struggle?

WILLIAMS: I think that really is the indication of what I was trying to do with Woodcock. That's why I set up that arrangement whereby Blackman says if you didn't have such nappy hair you'd be White. That was the precise arrangement. Instead of these people getting one of these big, bushy Afros, they ought to go back and get conks and be like the man and plant some bombs and things.

CASH: You suggested Africa as a possible place for Blacks to prepare themselves for guerilla warfare. Would not your suggestion, if taken seriously by Blacks, also be a warning for Whites, who may be in a position to repress black people?

WILLIAMS: Okay. But my feeling is that we tend to underestimate the ability of the white man to know what's going on. I think he knows exactly what's going on. The other thing is that in spite of the rhetoric about Africa and the possibility about moving to Africa and so on, I really can't see that happening immediately for two reasons: I think black Americans are still too much American. The other reason is that in order for this really to work black African leaders have to take the initiative and say we need, for example, five hundred teachers, and set up contractural deals so that five hundred black teachers can go to Africa and teach. I know of no such deal that's going on. That's only an example. There's a need for engineers, communications experts, and what have you. These things have not been dealt with in terms that could be considered beneficial to us. So the failure on the part of African leaders and the failure, not the failure but the sort of tacit acknowledgement that no matter how bad the situation is in America, black Americans are still Americans—I think that's what's holding us up.

CASH: There is a confrontation between the Blacks and the Indians in which the Indians chide the black man for joining the white soldiers against the Indians while Blacks would not fight the white man. No doubt you see this as another one of those ironies of history?

WILLIAMS: Yes, it is essentially correct. But there must somewhere be—they're starting to come out now—records of the number of Blacks who fought with the Seminoles, when Jackson finally went in there and tried to massacre everybody. It is, I suppose, one of the more pathetic moments in our history. Black folks were used. You want a job, you want to get in off the street, we'll put you out here in the plains and you can kill Indians or they can kill you. And, it worked out fairly well.

CASH: I was fascinated by the way you combined the fact and the fiction and how the novel seems to have an aura of the surreal. What do you think about the conclusion? Some reviewers called it a horrifying and shocking ending. Do you think that ending might detract from the book on the one hand, or it might increase the sales of the book?

WILLIAMS: I hadn't thought about it. I believe in books that have solid endings, that say something, you know. I suffer from criticism of being melodramatic because of that. The end of the novel is the end of the novel, not on page twenty-five or whatever. My editor had some pressure from the publishers for me to either drop the last section or set it apart because it was tied in to the chapter before. I said that's ridiculous. I'm not dropping it. If you want me to put in another section or chapter, I'd do that. And we both agreed that it'd make the book stronger just by standing alone, and people who raised protest obviously hadn't anticipated that at all. But there it is, all by itself, instead of merging. Additionally, I don't know how you could handle it any other way in a book like that. I'd not, certainly, try anything so trite as to have an uprising in Viet Nam, you know. You just fly over and napalm everybody—either that or the kinds

159

of things that are going on at these army bases. No, I just felt it had to be big and involving the whole military political situation. And you get into that if you start talking about missile sites and sub-sea floor sites and crap like that. They don't think niggers know anything about that—really don't.

CASH: To get to a point that's a little off from the book but still relevant, I think; you often mention that you don't review the reviews. Do you find yourself, then, paying any more or less attention to critiques, probably verbal, that might come from your immediate family, like your wife and sons?

WILLIAMS: I can't help but pay attention. The ones that come from the family are usually favorable so I just take my little pat on the back and that's that. But people will call and say "gee, that was a great review" or people will call and say "what was that guy trying to do to you in that review" and things like that; so that by osmosis, pretty much, you get some ideas of what these reviews are all about without reading them specifically yourself. And, perhaps, you can pick up nuances yourself which other people haven't. And then it depends on whether you know the reviewer. Like, take the first review that came in which Lori [his wife] read; that critic is always calling me paranoid; so that the turn of his review, judging from Lori's response, was more or less expected. And what sort of supports my idea of not reading these damned things is that these people are so damned consistent. There're no surprises in any of them.

CASH: Would you object, therefore, to my getting Dennis' [his second son] reaction to *Captain Blackman*?

WILLIAMS: No. I wanted the book to be very important to him because he's got a very low draft number and if he wasn't in school his ass would have been gone.

CASH: [Taking Dennis aside (he's now a senior at Cornell), I asked him the following question.] What do you think of *Captain Blackman*?

DENNIS: I liked it. I think it came off pretty well. It's not a safe book by any standards. Whereas say *The Man Who Cried I Am* was politically unsafe, of course, literarily it was on better ground. But *Captain Blackman* is politically even more unsafe because it deals with the whole course of history. It's even, in a sense, more radical. And literarily it's also radical because of the techniques used and everything. And it's very touchy the way it's going to work out. And the whole dream thing—the going back into the past—I stopped trying to make it make sense and just let it go. Because the dream thing is plausible, I guess. But it really is sort of not necessary; I know he was telling me once how he was trying to work out the technique. What he was going to do was use ghosts. Characters that go through time were going to be treated as ghosts. That seems pretty good too. It's sort of like once Blackman's consciousness first goes back and these alter egos are created, they sort of have a life of their own, for they seem to exist for long periods of time in the past. I think there are about six or seven different Blackmans. Another thing I was thinking about the other day, the dialogue is really good, like in the Cadences sections. For example, you have men sitting around the conference tables in war rooms making the plans. Some of the dialogue was based, I suppose, on records, and documents and transcripts. I don't know how actual all the dialogue is supposed to be. It's the kind of thing that some unbelievers might consider just pure fantasy or fiction. Then the idea of this dialogue of American and European generals sitting around and talking about what to do with the Blacks—you know, I'm just sure it's going to blow a lot of people's minds. And this kind of thing is not funny. As I've said, books of this type might be satirical, expected to be tongue-in-cheek or something like that, but it's absolutely serious. It's not meant to be taken as fantasy or as a joke. And whether people believe the dialogue to be fact or fiction really does not make that much difference to the overall effect of the story. The ending, by the way, adds a little extra punch, summarizes everything, gives a little hope, too.

There are times when it seems that he wanted certain facts put in there and you can see he's going to get them in one way or another. You can see how things are manipulated—battles, periods of war—to get to certain instances. I guess the whole World War II thing is concentrated on Tombolo where the white soldiers wipe out the black soldiers in the swamps. Again by that point, you've had enough of battles that you really don't care if the whole history of the war focuses on that specific. The flow of the book, though—it comes off.

CASH: [Returning to Williams.] In *This Is My Country Too*, you referred to—in an interview with Arthur Schlesinger, Jr.—you referred to him as a "writer-historian" and you call yourself a "writer," merely. Don't you think that now you deserve the twin title also?

WILLIAMS: Damn right! [Laughter]

Selected Bibliography

Works by John A. Williams, arranged chronologically

The Angry Ones, first published by Ace, 1960.
Night Song, first published by Farrar, Straus, Cudahy, 1961.
The Angry Black (editor), Lancer, 1962.
Africa: Her History, Lands and People, Lancer, 1963.
Sissie, first published by Farrar, Straus, Giroux, 1963.
The Protectors (under pseudonym, J. Dennis Gregory, with Harry T. Anslinger), Farrar, Straus, Giroux, 1964.
This Is My Country Too, New American Library, 1965.
Beyond the Angry Black, (editor) first published by Cooper Square, 1966.
The Man Who Cried I Am, first published by Little Brown, 1967.
Sons of Darkness, Sons of Light, first published by Little, Brown, 1969.
The King God Didn't Save, first published by Coward-McCann, 1970.
The Most Native of Sons, Doubleday, 1970.
Captain Blackman, Doubleday, 1972.
Flashbacks, Doubleday, 1973.

Articles, Reviews, Essays

B.,C.A. "An Angry Look at Life." *Buffalo Evening News,* 25 November 1961.
Baker, Houston A. Review of *Flashbacks. Black World,* October 1973.
Boroff, David. "Blue Note for Bigotry." *Saturday Review,* 30 March 1963.
Bouise, Oscar. Review of *Night Song. Best Sellers,* 1 December 1961.
Bowden, Ramona. "Time Said Short for Racial 'Evolution.' " *Syracuse Post-Standard,* 25 March 1968.
Bowser, Hallowell. "A Season of Discontent." *Saturday Review,* 6 October 1962.
Brooks, Gwendolyn. "Willing to Grapple on Life's Own Terms" *Chicago Sun-Times,* 31 March 1963.
Buckler, Ernest. "Rendezvous with Truth." *The New York Times Book Review,* 2 June 1963.
Buckmaster, Henrietta. "He Gives Anger Definition." *Christian Science Monitor,* 7 August 1969.
Cash, Earl A. Review of *Captain Blackman. Negro History Bulletin,* November, 1972.
Cook, Bruce. "Writers in Midstream: John Williams & James Baldwin." *The Critic,* February-March 1963.
"Courier Book Shelf." *Pittsburgh Courier,* 23 February 1963.
Cowan, Paul. "The Diary of a Writer." *The New York Times Book Review,* 6 May 1973.
Davis, George. "A Revolutionary War Soldier in Vietnam." *The New York Times Book Review,* 21 May 1972.
Dollen, Charles. Review of *The King God Didn't Save. Best Sellers,* September, 1970.
Feather, Review of *Night Song. Downbeat,* 4 January 1962.
Fleischer, Leonard. Review of *Captain Blackman. Saturday Review,* 13 May 1972.
Fleming, Robert E. "The Nightmare Level of *The Man Who Cried I Am.*" *Contemporary Literature,* Spring 1973.
Goran, Lester. "Humans Within Their Personality." *Chicago Tribune,* 31 March 1963.

Henderson, David. "The Man Who Cried I Am: A Citizen." *Black Expression*. Ed. Addison Gayle, Jr. New York: Weybright and Talley, 1969.

Hentoff, Nat. "Second-Class Citizenship: No Room 'to Behave Even Nominally Like a Man.' " *New York Herald Tribune*, 14 April 1963.

Kirschenbaum, Blossom. "Prix de Rome: The Writing Fellowship Given by the American Academy of Arts and Letters in conjunction with the American Academy in Rome, 1951-1963." Diss. Brown University 1972.

Lea, George. "A Jazz Journey." *Chicago Sun-Times*, 15 October 1961.

Long, Margaret. "A Negro Theme—Brutal, Tender." *Atlanta Journal-Constitution*, 15 October 1961.

Moon, Eric. Review of *Captain Blackman*. *Library Journal*, 1 May 1972.

Moran, William. "Novel Bares of Stark Color Conflict." *Columbia Missourian*, November 1961.

Neuhaus, Richard J. "Martin Luther King's Second Assassination." *New York Review of Books*, 8 October 1970.

Peavey, Charles D. "The Black Revolutionary Novel: 1899-1969." *Studies in the Novel*, 3, No. 2 (1971).

Powers, Dennis. "A Family's Journey Into the Past Is Rewarding Reading." *Oakland Tribune*, 20 January 1963.

Quigley, Martin. "Barriers That Do Not Melt Away." *St. Louis Globe-Democrat*, 9 December 1961.

Ray, David. "Eloquent, Bitter, First-Rate Novel." *Chicago News*, 3 April 1963.

Redding, J. Saunders. "Crazy, Man! Gone!" *New York Herald Tribune*, 26 November 1961.

S., N. "A Gem of a New Novel on Music (Jazz), People (Negro and White)." *People's World*, 13 January 1962.

Sheed, Wilfred. "Race War Novel, with a Cast of Thousands." *Book World*, 29 June 1969.

Spearman, Walter. "John Williams' Characters Create 'Human Heart in Conflict with Self.' " *The Rocky Mount Telegram*, 21 April 1963.

Starke, Catherine Juanita. *Black Portraiture in American Fiction*. New York: Basic Books, 1971.

"Two Negroes Write Protest Novels." *Albany Times Union*, 3 February 1963.

Walcott, Ronald. "*The Man Who Cried I Am*: Crying in the Dark." *Studies in Black Literature*, 3, No. 1 (1972).

Weigel, Jr., James. "Marginal Jazz World." *Louisville Courier Journal*, 7 January 1962.

West, Richard. "Inside Dope." *Manchester Guardian*, 10 May 1962.

Wheeler, Robert. "Individual Lives Measure the Meaning of Change." *Kansas City Star*, 5 May 1963.

"Williams Publishes History of Africa." *World*, 24 March 1964.

INDEX

Africa: Her History, Lands and People, 11–12, 26, 127
Amistad I, 28, 105, 144
Angry Black, The, 91, 118, 153
Angry Ones, The, 6, 33–46, 61, 78, 92, 94, 97, 100, 102, 104, 117, 124, 127, 132, 151, 152, 153
Anslinger, Harry J., 12, 13
Atlantic Monthly, The, 93

Baldwin, James, 4, 44, 60, 92, 99, 105, 144, 147
Beck, Robert, 4
Beyond the Angry Black, 118
Black Boy, 26, 91
Black Heroes in World History, 12
Black History: Lost, Stolen, or Strayed, 12
Black musicians, 131–132
Black Studies, 148
Black Thunder, 123, 127, 155
Blake, 1
Bontemps, Arna, 123, 155
Brooks, Gwendolyn, 118

Captain Blackman, 91, 105, 115, 117–124, 126, 128, 139, 154–162
Chesnutt, Charles, 3
Choice, The, 127
Clarke, John Henrick, 155, 156
Clotel, 1
Confessions of Nat Turner, The, 146, 155
Cool Ones, The, 40, 117, 119

Daily Mirror, 59
David McKay Co., 40, 43
Dostoevsky, Fyodor, 1, 5

Douglass, Frederick, 146
Dreiser, Theodore, 1, 75
Dunbar, Paul Laurence, 3

Ellison, Ralph, 3, 67, 92, 118

Faulkner, William, 148
Fire Next Time, The, 60
Flashbacks, 28–30, 62, 128

Graves, Robert, 123
Greenlee, Sam, 137
Gregory, J. Dennis, 12
Griffin, John Howard, 92, 147, 148

Himes, Chester, 28, 105, 129, 137, 147, 153
Holiday, 15, 17, 93, 152
Holiday, Billie, 13, 14
Homes, John Clellon, 47
Horn, The, 47
Howells, William Dean, 3
Hyman, Stanley Edgar, 3

I, Claudius, 123
Imperium in Imperio, 1, 127

Jet, 16
John Reed Club, 26
Johnson, James Weldon, 3
Joyce, James, 1, 5

Kelley, William Melvin, 5

165

Killens, John O., 5, 137, 147
Kimball, Richard A., 61, 63, 64, 67
King Alfred Plan, 106, 127
King God Didn't Save, The, 18–25, 113, 118, 128
King, Jr., Martin Luther, 18–25, 105, 108N, 109, 118, 128, 156
Kirschenbaum, Blossom, 61

Life and Loves of Mr. Jiveass Nigger, 145
Locke, Alain, 158
Lowry, Malcolm, 90

Mailer, Norman, 147
Malamud, Bernard, 148
Malcolm X, 19, 28, 105, 106, 108N
Man Who Cried I Am, The, 61, 93, 97–108, 109, 118, 127, 132, 136, 138, 139, 141, 143–144, 145, 146, 153, 156, 160
Mark of Oppression, 95N
McKay, Claude, 3
Moody's Squad, 91, 117–118
Most Native of Sons, The, 25–28, 99, 118, 128

Native Son, 26, 27
"Navy black", 118
Negro in the Making of America, The, 12
Negro Market Newsletter, 9, 151
New York Times, The, 59, 69, 70, 140, 141
Night Song, 47–71, 94, 102, 103, 127, 136, 144, 152, 153
Nugget, 62

O'Conner, Flannery, 53
Omni-American, The, 45N
One for New York, 40–42, 153

Pan-Africanism, 135–136
Parker, Charlie, 13, 14, 28, 48, 57, 59, 154

Paton, Alan, 147, 148
Playboy, 93
Prix de Rome, 29, 61–70, 73, 94, 105
Protectors, The, 12–14

Racial Attitudes of American Presidents, The, 120
Reader's Digest, 17
Reed, Ishmael, 5, 137
Robbe-Grillet, Alain, 147
Russell, Ross, 47

Savage Holiday, 27
Schuyler, George S., 89
Sinkler, George, 120
Sissie, 39, 68, 73–95, 104, 110, 118, 127, 140, 141, 153
Sisyphus, 56
"Son in the Afternoon", 91–93
Sons of Darkness, Sons of Light, 109–115, 118, 127, 133–134, 135, 136, 137–138
Sound, The, 47
Spook Who Sat by the Door, The, 127
Steinbeck, John, 14–15, 16–17, 18
Styron, William, 146, 155

This Is My Country Too, 15–18, 23, 37–38, 49, 92, 93, 104, 118, 127, 161
Thurman, Wallace, 3
Toomer, Jean, 3
Travels with Charley, 14–15, 17, 127, 152

Under the Volcano, 90
U.S. Commissioner of Narcotics, 12, 14

Violent Bear It Away, The, 53

"We Regret to Inform You That", 29, 62–70
William Styron's Nat Turner, 155

Williams, Dennis, 33, 160–161
Williams, Gregory, 33
Williams, John Henry, 6
Williams, Lori, 160
Williams, Ola, 6

Wright, Richard, 3, 4, 25–28, 90–91, 99, 100, 105, 126, 147

Yerby, Frank, 4
Yette, Samuel, 127